The Use of Principle

OLIVER ^{Piers} STUTCHBURY

THE USE OF
PRINCIPLE

THE BOYDELL PRESS
LONDON AND IPSWICH

THE BOYDELL PRESS LIMITED
LONDON AND IPSWICH

P.O. Box 24
Ipswich IP1 1JJ
Suffolk

First published 1973

Printed in Great Britain by
The Anchor Press Ltd, and bound by
Wm. Brendon & Son Ltd, both of Tiptree, Essex

ISBN 0 85115 020 9

Contents

Chapter		Page
	Preface	7
I	Patterns of Purposive Behaviour	9
II	The Truth-Value of Unconfined Weak Comparisons	27
III	Universality and Related Matters	39
IV	Strong Comparisons	51
V	Principles	67
VI	Moral Principles	80
VII	Rival Theories	97
VIII	Choice	104
	Complete Summary	107
	References	112
	Index	115

Preface

My aim in this book is to give, using the smallest number of unusual posits* (i.e. coining as few new technical terms) as I can, a sufficient answer to a philosophical puzzle which may be stated in a number of different ways. What is the difference between a moral principle and other sorts of principle? How do we come to distinguish between moral principles and others? How should one distinguish between moral principles and others? The first way of stating the problem makes it seem as if a descriptive account is what is needed; the second, an historical investigation; the third, an evaluative inquiry. Which is it to be? This, indeed, is part of the problem.

My central thesis is that the distinctive mark of moral principles is that they are not justified, nor do we come to justify them, nor should we seek to justify them, in terms of their conduciveness to some desired end. In this they are unlike other principles which we (quite rightly) justify because they are more likely to produce the result we desire than any alternative principle of which we are apprised.

I began to construct the argument contained in this book in 1950, during my final year at Cambridge. I submitted the first version (unsuccessfully) as a dissertation for Fellowship of my College. In the twenty years following, I have recast the material from time to time. It has appeared in a thesis for the degree of Ph.D. at London University (1963) and in lectures I

* posit = concept. I think I am using the word in precisely the same sense as I understand Quine to be using it in 'Two Dogmas of Empiricism', Essay II in *From a Logical Point of View*, Harvard University Press, 1953.

gave as a visiting Professor of Philosophy at the University of Colorado in 1965.

My fundamental debt to the published work of C. L. Stevenson, S. E. Toulmin, R. M. Hare and philosophers of the prescriptivist school of moral philosophy will be obvious from the text. The philosophers to whom I know I am indebted for specific ideas are mentioned in the body of the book. My best thanks are due to Ralph Instone for correcting the proofs and to John High for compiling the Index.

My argument is now as nearly right as I am ever likely to get it, and different enough from what anyone else has written to make me feel that it is worth publishing.

139, Old Church Street,
London, SW3 6EB.
December 1972

CHAPTER ONE

Patterns of Purposive Behaviour

1. *Purposive behaviour*

IT is a contingent fact (i.e. a matter of experience) about anyone who is not incapacitated that, at least during some part of his life, he sets out to accomplish tasks, to produce results, to reach goals, to pursue ends, and to achieve ambitions. I do not want to distinguish between these different ways of describing what I shall call 'purposive behaviour'. Even in the same individual, purposive behaviour may be directed towards very different results in quite a short time span. John Doe (a variable) may have breakfast in the morning to assuage his hunger, start his car in order to get to work, go to work to fulfil his obligations to his employer, visit his banker to secure overdraft facilities, play a round of golf to exercise himself, go to a sentimental film to indulge his emotions, have a whisky and soda to induce euphoria, put on different clothes to please a girl friend, fall on his knees to worship God, and go to bed to refresh himself for the next day. The list can be expanded indefinitely.

Purposive behaviour is not necessarily directed towards one aim. When John Doe has a whisky and soda, he may not only be anxious to induce euphoria, but also to gratify an acquaintance who has offered him the drink. He thus 'kills two birds with one stone'. When he goes to work, he may not only be fulfilling his obligations to his employers, he may be acting in accordance with a long-term ambition to serve his articles, pass his examinations and become a qualified professional man. Such a line of purposive behaviour will, of necessity, take him years to accomplish. While it is being pursued he may, consistently with his ambition, seek other long-term as well as short-term goals. He may go to Mass regularly on Sundays with a view to becoming one with God in the next world. He may play golf and practise his iron shots with a view to winning the Captain's Cup in the annual competition. He may also abandon the pursuit of an ambition in the middle. He may, during his articles, be offered a job by some employer which is sufficiently attractive to induce him to give up his projected professional career altogether and make new plans.

Nor is purposive behaviour an effort which is confined to an individual acting on his own. John Doe may combine with Richard Roe (another variable) in a joint enterprise to win the Club Foursomes. During his life he may get married, and he and his wife may together buy a house and start bringing up a family. He may combine with a team of people which is engaged in some joint scientific or commercial enterprise. He may join a political party with a view, in concert with others, to bringing into existence a brave new world.

It is sometimes difficult for a person to define his purpose or aim with any clarity. Someone who starts his car and takes his family out for a drive on Sunday afternoon may do it to give his children a treat, or to give his wife a break, or because he likes driving, or because he wants to get somewhere where he can do something else, or because he wants to show off his wealth, or because he cannot stand the mess indoors any longer. Or he may kill several birds with one stone by doing this same thing from a mixture of motives. Or he may pretend that he is giving his wife a break, when he really wants to show off his new car.

To talk of someone's 'motive' in doing something is to presuppose that he is engaged in purposive behaviour. There are other words which we use in the same context as when, in some varieties of purposive behaviour, we use the word 'pretext' to indicate that someone is (or may be) deliberately misleading us as to his real aim in doing something. For we may delude ourselves about our own motives to a grotesque extent. Some psychiatrists aver that behaviour indicating a need to acquire a valuable stamp collection may simply be a way of sublimating a primitive desire on the part of someone to collect his own excreta; that a schoolmaster caning a pupil may be indulging his sexual passions; that a hoodlum breaking up a telephone kiosk may be motivated by hatred of his father. However this may be, we all know the situation in which we pretend to want to achieve some result (which has no appeal to us) personally but which we do in order to please someone else whose pleasure we desire; as when we pretend to our aged relation that we enjoy mowing her lawn. My point is that a person's aims may be other than they appear to be, even than what they appear to him to be.

May I stress what I am *not* saying? I am not saying that, at every moment of his life, John Doe is necessarily pursuing purposive behaviour, even if he does not know what his goal is. A great deal of human conduct is purposeless or aimless. Even the most disciplined of us has many periods in his life when he is doing nothing, or marking time, or just messing about. Some people rarely seem to do anything with a sense of purpose; although, human nature being what it is, these people seem also to have a tendency eventually to take to the bottle with a sense of mission. Nor am I making the judgment that people *ought* to pursue purposive behaviour. At this stage in my argument I wish to try to be as neutral as I can about what people ought or ought not to do.

In any human being's life there is a wide spectrum between purposive and aimless behaviour. All I am arguing is that most people, at least during some parts of their lives, set out to accomplish tasks or to produce results or to reach goals or to pursue ends or to achieve ambitions: in other words, they engage in purposive behaviour. The simplest way to decide whether certain conduct is purposive behaviour or whether it is pointless behaviour is to imagine that the agent is asked: 'Why are you doing that?' or, 'What are you doing that for?' or, 'Are you doing that on purpose?' and that he answers: 'I am trying to . . . or I am doing this in order to . . .' or 'I am doing this on purpose.' Alternatively he may answer: 'Nothing!' or, 'I don't know.' Direct evidence like verbal answers to questions may be unavailable (or suspect), but where an observer is prepared to commit himself to a statement that the agent is trying to achieve something that agent will be engaging in purposive behaviour for the purpose of my argument.

It is immaterial that a person is pursuing different aims at the same time, or that he is deluded about what his real purpose is, or even that he is deceiving me about his goal. Provided he or someone else is prepared to state what he is trying to do, he is engaged in what I shall call purposive behaviour. A 'principle', the term I am concerned with in this book, is one which is confined to purposive behaviour; and, moreover, to purposive behaviour of a special sort.

SUMMARY: In classifying human activity, one can distinguish between purposive and aimless behaviour; the distinctive mark of purposive behaviour is that it is directed towards accomplishing tasks, producing results, reaching goals, pursuing ends and achieving ambitions.

2. *Looking, Talking and Philosophising*

It will clear the air if we look at three kinds of behaviour and ponder where each of them occurs in the spectrum between purposive and aimless behaviour.

During this present century, a technique of operating on persons with a certain rare form of blindness has been mastered. In consequence some patients born blind have received sight late in life and the testimony they give of what it is like learning to see shows us how lucky normal people are to acquire this skill in infancy without trouble. These patients report that, to begin with, the experience of opening their eyes is painful: they can see only a spinning mass of lights and colours. For weeks and months after beginning to see, patients can only with great difficulty distinguish between the simplest shapes, such as triangles and squares. It takes them at least a month to learn the names of even a few objects; and one man having learned to name an egg, a potato, and a cube of sugar when he saw them, could not name them when they were put in yellow light. The lump of sugar was successfully named when on the table, but not when hung up in the air by a piece of thread.

In any normal child's infancy, looking involves *learning*. What the previously blind man lacks according to J. Z. Young (*BBC Reith Lectures, 1950*) is the 'store of rules in the brain, rules usually learnt by the long years of exploration with the eyes during childhood'. We do not yet know what these rules are: 'probably learning to move the eyes in certain ways is an important part of the process'. Nor is the learning-to-see process one which normal people necessarily ever perfect. Very few Europeans can, when first observing them, distinguish between individual members of the Chinese race with the ease with which they can distinguish between Europeans, and *vice versa*. But such a skill can often be acquired with practice. 'In all sensation', writes Medawar, 'we pick and choose, interpret, seek and impose order, and devise and test hypotheses about what we witness. Sense data are taken, not merely given: we *learn* to perceive.'*[1] 'The brain of each of us', says Young, 'does literally create his or her own world.'

Although it has claims to be called purposive behaviour on my definition, looking is something which, when we have our eyes open, we cannot choose not to do. Or, perhaps more important, looking is a skill in which we do not ordinarily need instruction from others in learning. In this it is to be sharply distinguished from talking. Thus Hunter Diack:[2]

It is a common assumption that a child's education really begins when he makes his first steps in reading. That is a fallacy. His first steps in reading may indeed fairly well coincide with the beginning of his formal education, but his basic education began long before that. Indeed it could be argued that in the years between twelve months and five years he makes a greater educational advance than he will make in any subsequent period of similar duration.

It is during that period that he breaks through the sound barrier, learns to speak effectively. At the beginning of that

* Figure references refer to those on pp. 112–13 at the end of the book.

period his behaviour bears considerable resemblance to that of a highly intelligent chimpanzee; by the end of that period that comparison becomes something like sacrilege.

In learning to speak the child is learning to think, to perceive, to classify his perceptual experiences, to enter into relationships with other human beings and to engage in all the other activities which set human beings so decisely apart from all the other inhabitants of this planet. It is through speech that the child acquires his store of meanings. Unless a word has been encountered in speech it will mean nothing or very little to him, even long after he has learned to read. Even with adults it is on the whole true to say that anyone who cannot put into his own spoken words anything that he has read has not understood it but has allowed the print to drift through his mind.

What peculiarly distinguishes man from the other primates is, it is agreed on all sides, his ability to use words in communicating with other human beings. People learn to see in order to be aware of what is around them. People learn to speak in order to be able to communicate more effectively with other people. The two activities differ in that learning to speak (unlike learning to see—in the normal child) requires assistance from someone else. In the communication of this assistance, a whole complex of words have been invented which have puzzling philosophical characteristics, and it is with this complex of words that I am concerned in this book.

For me, the study of philosophy is a variety of purposive behaviour. If, when engaged in philosophising, I should be asked. 'Why are you reading that?' or, 'What are you writing that for?' my answer (following Quine) [3] would be: 'I am making an effort to "get clearer on things*"'. But this is not necessarily so for other philosophers. One may hold the view that he philosophizes to help him to know how 'to live the good life' (whatever

* 'Getting clearer on things' I take to be no more than an aesthetic pleasure, akin to that experienced by scientists when first they perceive the simplicity of the right hypothesis; or by mathematicians when they first appreciate the elegance of a proof and know it to be true. 'To get clearer on things' is equivalent to to *get the hang* of things' in a less sophisticated operation.

he may mean by this). Indeed, there is no absurdity in holding the view that philosophising is a species of messing about—albeit of a rare and absorbing kind. But in that event it is rather pointless. Precisely so, for then it has no aim. Doing philosophy is not purposive behaviour to a person who holds such a view.

In the previous section I said that I wished to try to be as neutral as I could about what people ought or ought not to do. But there is one sphere in which it is, in practice, impossible to be neutral. In my argument I am using words. However hard I try I cannot be neutral about how words ought to be used—even if it is only to indicate how I shall be using them myself, for to indicate how I shall be using words carries (in some contexts) a covert implication that this is how they *ought* to be used. A great deal of philosophy (it need hardly be mentioned) centres round this far from trivial question about how a word *ought* to be used, and this is sometimes produced as evidence of philosophy's uselessness. To some of us, however, this is evidence of its central importance in getting clearer on things.

SUMMARY: Speaking is a variety of purposive behaviour. For some people, philosophising is a variety of purposive behaviour directed to the aim of getting clearer on things. To this end, much may depend on how individual words ought to be used.

3. *Weak Comparisons*

One contingent fact about purposive behaviour is that similar purposive behaviour *recurs*. Little John Doe is not the only child who has to learn to communicate in words. Little Richard Roe has to do so too. Similar purposive behaviour recurs not only in the lifetime of different individuals, but in the life of the same individual. When John Doe has breakfast one morning to assuage his hunger, it is not the unique occasion on which he has breakfast. In all probability he has had breakfast the previous day, and will have breakfast on the morrow. (In the following pages I make a lot of this trivial business of having breakfast, for what we have for breakfast may well be one of the first conscious choices we make each day.) If John Doe sets out to win the Captain's Cup in the annual competition at his golf club, he may try to win it in a number of different years. Moreover, John Doe may not be unique in this latter respect; and Richard Roe and many other people eat breakfast every morning, and go in for the Captain's Cup too.

I shall call purposive behaviour directed towards the *same* task, result, goal, aim, end, ambition (whatever you like to call it and I shall tend to call it 'result') by the same or different persons a 'pattern of purposive behaviour'. It is with patterns of purposive behaviour that I am concerned from now on. So I am not interested in an individual's day by day plan to do specific things, like the breakfast John Doe has on Thursday, 18 May, 1967, or little Richard Roe's learning to speak. But I am interested so far as either John Doe or Richard Roe himself, or someone else, tries to reach the *same* result. I am, in other words, interested from now onwards in patterns of purposive behaviour that recur both in an individual's own lifetime and in the lives of other individuals. This is what I meant when I said at the end of the first section of this Chapter that I was concerned with the terms associated with a 'special sort' of purposive behaviour.

It is a contingent fact about any pattern of purposive behaviour that different performances of the pattern can be compared by some person both with his own performance at another time and with another's performance of the same pattern at the same time or at different times. A performance of a pattern of purposive behaviour is usually (and ought to be) compared by someone with another performance of the same pattern on its success in achieving the result at which that pattern of purposive behaviour is aimed.

There are monumental difficulties connected with making some comparisons which I shall, eventually, touch upon. But there are no difficulties connected with making others, and I shall begin by investigating these. It is only if we are clear how uncomplicated comparisons are used that we can hope to be clear about how complicated comparisons function in our language. There are no difficulties involved in comparing little John Doe's performance of the pattern of purposive behaviour involved in speaking with little Richard Roe's performance, if little John Doe can talk, but little Richard Roe cannot talk. Little John Doe's performance is *better than* little Richard Roe's. John Doe's performance of the pattern of purposive behaviour involved in winning the Captain's Cup in the annual competition in 1967 was better than Richard Roe's performance if John Doe won the Captain's Cup, but Richard Roe did not. Richard Roe's performance of the pattern of purposive behaviour involved in passing his Bar Finals was better than John Doe's, if Richard Roe passed, but John Doe did not. And so on.

Comparisons between performances can be made in a bewildering variety of ways. I shall begin by investigating the form of 'weak comparison' [4] of which I have just given instances—the form in which one performance is said to be *better than* another. 'To compare' in this sense means 'to make a comparative judgment about two performances of a pattern of purposive behaviour, that one is better than the other'. I shall use the technical term 'weak comparison' for the posit derivable from this long verbal phrase.

From a weak comparison of two different performances of a pattern of purposive behaviour it is but a step (and an unimportant step from a *moral* philosopher's point of view) to a weak comparison of classes of performances. Set out formally, the form of confined weak comparison I shall begin by investigating may be expressed as follows (I call it 'confined', for a reason which will appear shortly):

COMPARISON (MARK I)

'For Agent X, action A is a better way of performing the pattern of purposive behaviour P than action B if he wants to achieve result R in circumstances (1) and (2).'—*Spokesman*.

It should be understood that the word 'better' in this context is not meant to convey any suggestion of moral approval. It means no more than 'efficacious'.

B   *17*

Let me give concrete examples of confined weak comparisons any of which might be used in an unremarkable day's passage.

The Nanny's comparison (Mark I)

Agent:	'For John Doe
Action A:	using the pot
Comparison:	is a better way of defecating than
Action B:	using his pants
Result R:	if he wants to stay clean
Circumstance (1):	in a house with main drainage
Circumstance (2):	which is not on fire.'
Spokesman:	—*John Doe.*

The Etymologist's comparison (Mark I)

Agent:	'For Richard Roe
Action A:	calling that stuff "spaghetti"
Comparison:	is a better way of communicating in words than
Action B:	calling it "bascotti"
Result R:	if he wants to be understood by people
Circumstance (1):	who are not members of the family and
Circumstance (2):	who have been to Italy.'
Spokesman:	—*Richard Roe.*

The Dietician's comparison (Mark I)

Agent:	'For John Doe
Action A:	swallowing a Prairie Oyster*
Comparison:	is a better way of having breakfast than
Action B:	eating porridge
Result R:	if he wants to assuage his hunger
Circumstance (1):	after a drinking bout
Circumstance (2):	in summer but not in winter.'
Spokesman:	—*John Doe.*

* Prairie Oyster (also called Mountain Oyster in America) is made differently in various parts of the world. Here is a well-known recipe: 2 teaspoonfuls each of Worcester Sauce and Brandy, 1 teaspoonful each of Vinegar and Tomato Ketchup; mix well, drop the yolk of a fresh egg in the glass, and add red pepper on top.

Patterns of Purposive Behaviour

The Mechanic's comparison (Mark I)

Agent:	'For Richard Roe
Action A:	using the starting handle
Comparison:	is a better way of starting a car than
Action B:	using the self-starter
Result R:	if he wants to avoid damaging the batteries
Circumstance (1):	in cold weather
Circumstance (2):	away from a maintenance depot.'
Spokesman:	—Richard Roe.

The Law Tutor's comparison (Mark I)

Agent:	'For John Doe
Action A:	going to a firm of law crammers
Comparison:	is a better way of learning the law than
Action B:	attending a university
Result R:	if he wants to pass his Bar Finals
Circumstance (1):	in the shortest time
Circumstance (2):	with the minimum of expense.'
Spokesman:	—John Doe.

The Logical Positivist's comparison (Mark I)

Agent:	'For Richard Roe
Action A:	avoiding the predicates "true" or "false" of statements other than tautologies and scientific hypotheses
Comparison:	is a better way of arguing than
Action B:	predicating truth or falsehood of such statements
Result R:	if he wants to make himself clear
Circumstance (1):	in talking to other philosophers
Circumstance (2):	at Joint Sessions of the Mind Association and the Aristotelian Society.'
Spokesman:	—Richard Roe.

The Probation Officer's comparison (Mark I)

Agent:	'For John Doe
Action A:	drinking a glass of whisky

Comparison: is a better thing to do than
Action B: taking drugs
Result R: if he wants to induce euphoria
Circumstance (1): when money is no object
Circumstance (2): in his youth.'
Spokesman: —*John Doe.*

The Musicologist's comparison (Mark I)
Agent: 'For Richard Roe
Action A: playing a harpsichord
Comparison: is a better way of performing any of Bach's
                    forty-eight Preludes and Fugues than
Action B: playing a piano
Result R: if he wants to please his audience
Circumstance (1): in Germany but not in the U.S.A.
Circumstance (2): in a small hall.'
Spokesman: —*Richard Roe.*

The Businessman's comparison (Mark I)
Agent: 'For John Doe
Action A: speaking the whole truth
Comparison: is a better way of behaving than
Action B: concealing a relevant fact
Result R: if he wants to get an overdraft from
                    his bank manager
Circumstance (1): which he may wish to enlarge
Circumstance (2): having once been a bankrupt.'
Spokesman: —*John Doe.*

The Aesthetician's comparison (Mark I)
Agent: 'For Richard Roe
Action A: wearing a tie of any colour other than
                    magenta
Comparison: is a better way of dressing than
Action B: wearing a magenta tie
Result R: if he wants to look fashionable

Circumstance (1): when he is wearing a pink shirt
Circumstance (2): made of silk not satin.'
Spokesman: —*Richard Roe.*

These are all examples of what I have called 'confined weak comparisons'. They occur only when performances of the same pattern of purposive behaviour recur or are likely to recur, but in one form or another they are used in an astonishingly varied range of human activities from mundane humdrum everyday pursuits (the Mechanic's comparison) to the higher reaches of philosophy (the Logical Positivist's comparison) and aesthetics (the Musicologist's comparison). One of the points I wish to make is that the way in which we use weak comparisons is the same whether we are engaged in some essentially frivolous choice like breakfasting with a hang-over, or whether we are making a solemn decision about whether or not to speak the truth.

Another way of making this same point is to say that, whether they concern earthy or lofty patterns of purposive behaviour, weak comparisons have the same logic. But if one says this, it is necessary to go rather more closely into what one means by the word 'logic'. Readers who persist with my argument until the end of the book will see that how I choose to use this word constitutes one of the cornerstones of my thesis, and so I shall try to be as explicit as possible.

To begin with it must be admitted that I am using the word with a much wider application than most mathematicians and philosophers would favour. I shall use 'logic' as a technical term in the following way: by two statements having the same logic I mean (a) that their truth-values are established by the same procedures, and (b) that the same principles of inference are employed in the use of the two.

By a 'principle of inference', I mean a rule, with the use of which and nothing else, the truth-value of a conclusion can be established from an examination of the truth-values of its premises.

In insisting that confined weak comparisons have the same

logic whether they are made about mundane humdrum everyday pursuits or about the higher reaches of philosophy or aesthetics, I am taking a line of argument, for the first time in this book, which is different from what many other philosophers would take. In my view it is in an examination of the logic of comparisons that an answer to the problem of the difference between moral principles and others is to be found.

SUMMARY: Purposive behaviour directed towards the same result recurs, both when engaged in by the same person and when engaged in by others. I shall call these recurrences separate performances of the same 'pattern of purposive behaviour'.

It is a contingent fact about two performances of the same pattern of purposive behaviour that they can be compared with one another on their success in achieving the result at which the pattern of purposive behaviour is aimed. I shall call a statement of the form set out below a 'confined weak comparison':

COMPARISON (MARK I)

'For agent X, action A is a better way of performing the pattern of purposive behaviour P than action B if he wants to achieve result R in circumstances (1) and (2).'—Spokesman.

Statements of this form have the same logic whether they are about earthy or lofty patterns of purposive behaviour.

4. Unconfined Weak Comparisons

When people make weak comparisons in the course of their daily lives some (or many) of the individual elements may be missing. For instance, one or both specifications of the circumstances, or the identification of the agent may be taken for granted from the particular context in which the weak comparison occurs. Or the individual elements may be assumed because of very generally followed conventions. Sometimes they are left vague through accident or through lack of clarity of expression. Sometimes they are just obscure or left deliberately vague. We will examine these vagaries in the next Chapter.

So far I have taken care that, in the examples I have given, the agent of my examples has been identical with the spokesman. Such weak comparisons may correctly be said to be subjective or peculiar to John Doe or Richard Roe as the case may be—and one may justifiably doubt whether they ever, in fact, occur. It is only (we need assume at this stage) for John Doe personally that calling the stuff 'spaghetti' is a better way of communicating in words than calling it 'bascotti', and it is only for him that, with a hangover, swallowing a Prairie Oyster is a better way of breakfasting than eating porridge. But there may also be weak comparisons which apply uniquely to a named agent or to a limited class of individuals, and which may be made by a spokesman who is not the same person as (or of the class of individuals including) the agent—and these do, in fact, occur. Thus:

The Prince of Wales's comparison

Agent:	'For the Prince of Wales
Action A:	attending only Church of England services
Comparison:	is a better way of discovering about religion than
Action B:	sampling other religious ceremonies
Result R:	if he wants peace of mind
Circumstance (1):	while he is in Northern Ireland
Circumstance (2):	before he is fifty years old.'
Spokesman:	—*Richard Roe.*

The Englishman abroad's comparison

Agent:	'For any Englishman
Action A:	speaking English in a loud voice
Comparison:	is a better way of communicating in words than
Action B:	talking French
Result R:	if he wants to be understood
Circumstance (1):	in the shortest possible time

Circumstance (2): while on holiday in France.'
Spokesman: —*any Frenchman.*

These may be called 'confined' weak comparisons and they apply uniquely to a named individual or to a particular class of individuals. From now on, by contrast, I am concentrating on comparisons in which the agent may be *anyone*. I shall then say that the weak comparison is 'unconfined'. Thus:

COMPARISON (MARK II)

'(For anyone) Action A is a better way of performing the pattern of purposive behaviour P than action B if one wants to achieve result R in circumstances (1) and (2).'—*Spokesman.*

Once again to give examples.

The Nanny's comparison (Mark II)
Agent: '(For anyone)
Action A: Using the pot
Comparison: is a better way of defecating than
Action B: using *one's* pants
Result R: if *one* wants to stay clean
Circumstance (1):   in a house with main drainage
Circumstance (2):   which is not on fire.'
Spokesman: —*John Doe.*

The Etymologist's comparison (Mark II).
Agent: '(For anyone)
Action A: Calling that stuff "spaghetti"
Comparison: is a better way of communicating in
                    words than
Action B: calling it "bascotti"
Result R: if *one* wants to be understood by people
Circumstance (1):   who are not members of the family and
Circumstance (2):   who have been to Italy.'
Spokesman: —*John Doe.*

And so on through the examples I have already given on pages 18–21: '(For anyone) Swallowing a Prairie Oyster is a better way of having breakfast . . .' etc.

The origin of these unconfined weak comparisons is not hard to surmise. It is a contingent fact that we are (all of us) often called upon to perform patterns of purposive behaviour of which we have had no, or inadequate, previous experience: of which we have no or inadequate *knowledge* (as we sometimes say). After all, someone must teach us how to speak. In these circumstances an unconfined weak comparison may provide us with guidance.

Unconfined weak comparisons may be treated as the weakest verbal link by which know-how can be communicated from one individual to another. They provide the verbal medium by which patterns of purposive behaviour can be taught and learnt, by which motor skills may be imparted from one person to another. It is my thesis that all the more sophisticated and complex verbal constructions (like 'principles') used in teaching and learning how to perform patterns of purposive behaviour can be constructed from this one basic posit.

My reason for beginning at this end (i.e. with 'better than') rather than opening the argument with 'right' or 'good' is set out clearly by Quine:[5] 'A predicate resists the comparative suffix except insofar as it is systematically vague or elliptical to begin with, gaining precision only in the comparative.' My argument is that 'good', 'right', etc., are systematically vague or elliptical in this way, and consequently any analysis or explanation of them will also be vague or elliptical. 'Better than', being more precise, is a simpler place to start.

Having introduced the concept of 'knowledge', I owe the reader some further elucidation of what I mean. A persistent sceptic can, without much effort, cast doubts upon Ryle's distinction between 'know-how' and 'know-that'[6] (on the difference between the kind of knowledge involved in someone's being able to tie a bow tie and someone's knowing that Charles I died on the scaffold) because the two shade into one another in some contexts. But for some purposes it is a useful distinction. The problems of moral philosophy with which I am concerned in this book are problems connected with know-how. It is part of my argument that many philosophers have made a fundamental mistake in applying to these problems techniques which are only useful in solving difficulties connected with know-that. Their mistake is that they seek to order fleeting concepts describing actions in the same moulds as tangible concepts describing material objects. The temptation to do this needs no elaboration, but it should be resisted.

SUMMARY: I will call a weak comparison in which the agent may be anyone, an 'unconfined weak comparison', to distinguish it from a weak comparison which is peculiar to one particular individual or class of individuals (a 'confined weak comparison'), thus:

COMPARISON (MARK II)

'(For anyone) Action A is a better way of performing the pattern of purposive behaviour P than action B if one wants to achieve result R in circumstances (1) and (2).'—Spokesman.

All the more complex verbal constructions used in teaching and learning how to perform patterns of purposive behaviour can be constructed from this one basic posit.

CHAPTER TWO

The Truth-Value of Unconfined Weak Comparisons

1. The Truth-Value of a Comparison

B Y saying of comparisons that they have the same logic, and defining logic in the way I have, I am committed to the view that comparisons have a truth-value: that they can, at the least, be 'true' or 'false' (I shall, indeed, argue that there are three possible truth-values of a comparison—but this can be left for the moment). But it is argued by some philosophers that comparisons cannot be true or false.

Comparisons, it is argued, are a species of value-judgment. Value-judgments are incurably subjective or flamboyantly emotive or essentially prescriptive and hence meaningless or nonsensical or both; or insofar as they are not, they acquire meaning from the Description-words [7] contained in them. So it is argued that it is 'misleading' to call comparisons true or false because to do so may delude some people into supposing that the truth-value of a comparison can be *proved* by the same sort of techniques and procedures that establish the truth-value of an arithmetical proposition or a scientific hypothesis.

To say that a certain course of action is 'misleading' is a covert way of saying that it is better not to do it. So the argument that I have to answer can itself be stated as a comparison: something like the Mark II version of the Logical Positivist's comparison: '(For anyone) avoiding the predicates "true" or "false" of statements other than tautologies and scientific hypotheses is a better way of arguing than predicating truth or falsehood of such statements if one wants to make oneself clear in talking to other philosophers.' But is it *true* that it is better not to talk in this way?

Many people would affirm (and I would agree with them) that certain statements can be validly inferred from a comparison. Exactly *what* can be validly inferred is a matter of some delicacy but that is not to say that nothing can. For example, the people who would argue that it is misleading to call comparisons true and false might well also argue as follows. If it is true that (1) a comparison is a species of value-judgment, and (2) it is better not to assign truth-values to value judgments, then one can validly derive (3) that it is better not to assign truth-values to comparisons from the conjunction of (1) and (2).

Now, the whole concept of 'inference' is dependent upon being able to assess the truth-value of a conclusion, from the truth-values of the premises of the argument and the validity of the relevant rule of inference. So, unless I can use the predicates 'true' and 'false' of comparisons, I cannot use the concept of inference in this context. It seems to me to be so obvious that one can properly speak of inferring (3) from the conjunction of (1) and (2) above, and so obvious that both (2) and (3) are comparisons, that it must be false to say that it is better not to assign truth-values to value-judgments.

If what I have argued about this is not true, then I need not be too worried, for the Logical Positivist's comparison will not be true either, for it, itself, is a value-judgment.

I am prepared to concede that there is a sense in which the use of the word 'true' when used of comparisons is more closely akin to its use in phrases like 'set true' and 'true friend', than to its use in phrases like 'true scientific hypothesis'. But this is not to concede that it is better not to predicate truth or falsehood of comparisons at all.

What I am arguing therefore is that the truth-value of a comparison can be established in certain circumstances by procedures which I shall outline, and, although these procedures may not be the same as are used in the case of scientific hypotheses or arithmetical theorems, this need not preclude us from predicating truth or falsehood of any comparison.

The Truth-Value of Unconfined Weak Comparisons

SUMMARY: It is false to suggest that it is better not to assign a truth-value to value-judgments.

2. Two Sorts of 'Inanity'

Suppose that neither John Doe nor Richard Roe wins the Captain's Cup in the annual competition in 1967, but both lose to their opponents in the first round, in the same conditions, with the same number of strokes. Would it then be *false* to say that John Doe's performance was better than Richard Roe's performance?

Suppose that neither John Doe nor Richard Roe pass their Bar Finals in May 1971, but that both of them fail, having had the same facilities for study and being of equal intelligence. Would it then be *false* to say that Richard Roe's performance was better than John Doe's?

In circumstances wherein both John Doe and Richard Roe are aiming at the same result, then (in my opinion) it would be *false* to say that either was better than the other—because both would be equally bad. But this illustrates the crucial importance of the result in assessing the truth-value of a comparison: if the result aimed at is different from what we had assumed, then the truth-value may be different.

Suppose that the result at which both John Doe and Richard Roe were aiming was not to win the Captain's Cup but to display good sportsmanship, and John Doe (but not Richard Roe) had lost his temper at the 18th and stumped off the green without shaking hands with his opponent. What then? Then it would be *true* to say Richard Roe's performance was better than John Doe's. Similarly with the Bar Finals illustration: both are equally bad. But if Richard Roe had been involved in a serious car accident the day before the examinations started and had only been discharged from hospital to allow him to sit the exams, then if the goal is to display courage in adversity, Richard Roe's performance can truly be said to be better than John Doe's.

It is to be remarked about these comparisons that they are either true or false depending upon the result at which the pattern of purposive behaviour is aimed. But suppose this result is so vague and nebulous as to be unidentifiable. Take the following examples of Mark II comparisons:

Christopher Robin's comparison

Action A:	'Stepping in the middle of each paving stone
Comparison:	is a better way of walking along the pavement than
Action B:	stepping on the cracks between them
Result R:	if one wants to achieve peace of mind
Circumstance (1):	when walking outside Buckingham Palace
Circumstance (2):	on a rainy day.'
Spokesman:	—John Doe.

The Loyalist's comparison

Action A:	'Standing up
Comparison:	is a better way of conducting oneself during the playing of one's National Anthem than
Action B:	sitting down
Result R:	if one wants to preserve the decencies of life
Circumstance (1):	in a democratic society
Circumstance (2):	in a public place.'
Spokesman:	—Richard Roe.

The Traditionalist's comparison

Action A:	'Shooting them on any day of the week except Sundays
Comparison:	is a better way of hunting wild animals than
Action B:	shooting them on Sundays
Result:	if one wants to do God's Will

Circumstance (1): when they are not vermin and
Circumstance (2): one is not hungry.'
Spokesman: —*John Doe.*

Is it true to say of these three comparisons that they are true or false, or even *could* be true or false? The difficulty centres round the identification of the three results at which they profess to be aimed. What is it to achieve peace of mind in the context of Christopher Robin's comparison? or, to preserve the decencies of life? or, to do God's Will if one is sceptical of finding His Will manifested? (I am disregarding, for the moment, those people who specify where one can find out God's Will.) Although some individuals may profess private intuitions of what it is to do these things, they may seem to many of us to be too vague to be useful as results at which patterns of purposive behaviour can, in practice, be aimed. It is for consideration whether the traditional utilitarian's aim—to maximise happiness for the maximum number of people—does not fall into the same category of being too vague to be useful.

I shall use a technical term to describe the truth-value of such a comparison: a comparison in which the identification of the result is so nebulous that it is impossible to say whether it could be true or false. I shall say of such a comparison that it is 'inane' (i.e. literally empty, void). We can all think of a very large number of inane comparisons of the following kind: (For anyone) opening the window is a better way of wasting time than shutting the door if one wants to confuse one's enemies in the next street in hot weather. The Goons used to make money out of such flights of fancy.

The examples I have so far given are of comparisons that are *inane as to result.* I would now like to identify another way in which comparisons may be inane. They may specify no recognisable course of action. Take the following examples of Mark II comparisons:

The Rosicrucian's comparison
Action A: 'Searching for experience

Comparison:	is a better way of conducting one's life than
Action B:	pursuing happiness
Result R:	if one wants to make a million pounds
Circumstance (1):	before one is fifty
Circumstance (2):	in a capitalist society.'
Spokesman:	—Richard Roe.

The Art Dealer's comparison

Action A:	'Keeping one's integrity
Comparison:	is a better way of choosing artists than
Action B:	developing one's personality
Result R:	if one wants to sell more than 200 pictures a year
Circumstance (1):	at a little gallery
Circumstance (2):	in Cork Street, London, W.1.'
Spokesman:	—John Doe.

The Archbishop's comparison

Action A:	'Praying to the Almighty
Comparison:	is a better way of addressing God than
Action B:	praying to the Trinity
Result R:	if one wants to unite the Methodists with the Church of England
Circumstance (1):	at Lambeth Palace
Circumstance (2):	in 1972.'
Spokesman:	—Richard Roe.

In none of these comparisons is the result anything but reasonably precise: making a million pounds, selling more than two hundred pictures a year, and uniting the Methodist with the Church of England in 1972, being specific goals.

But how does one differentiate between 'searching for experience' and 'pursuing happiness', between 'keeping one's integrity' and 'developing one's personality', or between 'praying to the Almighty' and 'praying to the Trinity'? In no way that I, for one, can see a difference.

32

These comparisons are *inane as to action*. But I do not need to differentiate between these two varieties of inanity. Comparisons which are inane cannot be either true or false.

So in my language, a comparison may have one of three truth-values: a comparison may be true, false or inane. For the reason that comparisons have a three-valued logic, it will be no surprise to find that the traditional rules which govern a two-valued logic, like the *modus ponendo ponens* and the *modus tollendo tollens* (which I shall elucidate later), etc., do not always yield valid inferences of comparisons.

Two statements have the same sort of logic if (among other things) their truth-values are established by the same procedures. By what procedure is the truth-value of a comparison established? My argument will start from a basic assumption:

A comparison should be assumed to be inane unless it can be established to be true or false.

This First Maxim in establishing the truth-value of a comparison will apply alike to lofty comparisons connected with whether it is better to tell the truth than to speak a lie, and to earthy comparisons about whether it is better to have an Alka Seltzer or a Prairie Oyster for breakfast with a hangover. They are all to be assumed to be neither true nor false, but void, empty or inane, unless it can be established that they are true or false.

SUMMARY: Where, in a comparison, the result at which the pattern of purposive behaviour is said to be aimed is too vague to be identifiable, or the alternative actions specified are indistinguishable, then I shall say of such a comparison that it is inane. So comparisons have a three-valued logic. The First Maxim in establishing the truth-value of a comparison is that it should be assumed to be inane unless it can be established to be true or false.

3. *Teleological Reasons*

Assuming then that comparisons are inane until they are proved otherwise, by what procedures can one establish their truth or falsehood?

In this connection is is important to bear in mind the distinction which Urmson[8] has made especially his own: the difference between the *setting* of standards of evaluation and *making use* of those standards. In the realm of action, what Urmson calls standards, I call comparisons. The procedures which are relevant in establishing its truth or falsehood when one *advances* (or sets) a comparison, are different from the procedures which are relevant in establishing its truth or falsehood (or its 'rightness' or 'wrongness' as one sometimes says in this context) when one *makes use* of a comparison. In the former situation, one is in the position of (what I have called) the spokesman to the comparison; in the latter one is the agent.

When a spokesman is advancing a comparison, a good reason he can give for saying that it is true is that the *consequences* of adopting it (or conforming to it) will achieve the result at which the pattern of purposive behaviour in question is aimed. A good reason which can be given in refutation of a principle is that the consequences of adopting it will *not* achieve the result at which the pattern of purposive behaviour in question is aimed; or that the consequences of conforming to a different comparison would conduce to the result more effectively.

When one is advancing the Etymologist's comparison to one's child, a good reason that one can give for its truth is that one will be understood if one calls that stuff 'spaghetti' (in the circumstances of the case) but not if one calls it 'bascotti'. Similarly, a good reason one could produce for showing that the Law Tutor's comparison was false would be evidence that no one who had been to a firm of law crammers had ever passed his Bar Finals. A good reason for saying that the Nanny's comparison is true is that (unless one defines the word 'clean' in an absurdly perverse way) someone who messes his pants does not stay clean.

Let us enshrine this truism about the consequences of adopting a comparison providing a good reason for justifying its truth-value, in a *Second Maxim*:

When advancing a comparison, one ought to establish its truth-value by showing that the consequences of adopting it would, or would not, conduce to the result at which the particular pattern of purposive behaviour in question is aimed.

Such reasons, based on the consequences of following a comparison, I will (following Broad[9]) call 'teleological reasons'. Pragmatists and utilitarians are to be distinguished by a belief that teleological reasons are the *only* reasons which one ought to take into account in assessing the truth-value of a comparison.

The Second Maxim applies equally to lofty and earthy comparisons. That it is better to speak the truth than to tell a lie can be justified by an appeal to the consequences of alternative ways of behaving in the same way as the comparison that it is better to swallow a Prairie Oyster than take an Alka Seltzer for breakfast with a hangover. Both comparisons have the same logic in this respect.

SUMMARY: The Second Maxim is that, when advancing a comparison, one ought to establish its truth-value by showing that the consequences of adopting it would, or would not, conduce to the result at which the particular pattern of purposive behaviour in question is aimed. 'Teleological reasons' (as I shall call these) justify lofty and earthy comparisons alike.

4. Received Reasons

The procedures which are relevant in establishing its truth or falsehood when one *advances* a comparison, are different from the procedures which are relevant in establishing its truth or falsehood when one *makes use of* a comparison. When one makes use of a comparison (i.e. when one is the agent), it is something about the spokesman which leads one (and ought to lead one) to believing that a comparison is true or false. So when one is an agent, a good reason for believing that a comparison is true is that everyone in a position to know agrees that it is true. *Per contra,* a good reason for believing that a comparison is false is that everyone in a position to know agrees that it is false.

The difficulties arise when spokesmen disagree, but for the moment we can leave aside this phenomenon. A good reason (if one is a beginner at communicating) for believing that it is true that it is better to call that stuff 'spaghetti' than 'bascotti' is that your parents, your siblings and all your acquaintances aver that it is better to call it 'spaghetti' than to call it 'bascotti' if you want to be understood by people who are not members of the family who have been to Italy. A good reason for believing that it is false that it is better to call that same stuff 'bascotti' than to call it 'spaghetti' is that all the experts (i.e. those who know how to communicate) agree that it is false. If someone were able to say that not only the A. J. Ayer of *Language, Truth & Logic* days, but also the current A. J. Ayer and Quine and Goodman and Malcolm and Strawson and Wisdom and Ryle and Hare and Popper and Braithwaite agreed on the truth of the Logical Positivist's comparison and that no philosopher of standing disagreed, then that person would be well on the way to having a cast iron reason for believing that the Logical Positivist's comparison was true.

Let us enshrine this truism about spokesmen (teachers, experts, professionals—whatever one likes to call them) in a *Third Maxim*:

When entertaining the idea of using a comparison, one ought to establish its truth or falsehood by taking the word of the experts in the particular pattern of purposive behaviour involved.

Such reasons, based on the guidance of others, I will call 'received reasons'. Authoritarians are to be distinguished (and I include in this description the more extreme type of Theist—God being the Supreme Expert) by a belief that received reasons are the only reasons one ought to take into account in establishing the truth-value of a comparison.

It may be argued that in my account of the Three Maxims one employs (and ought to employ) in establishing the truth-value of a comparison, I ignore an important distinction. The reason, it may be argued, that a theorem of mathematics is true is the proof of the theorem. The fact that good mathematicians tell one that it is true is a reason for believing that it is true, but not a reason why it is true.

Similarly with regard to comparisons. The agreement of the experts may be a reason for deciding to adopt a comparison (i.e. to treat it as if it were true), not a reason why it is true. My maxims, it is argued, confuse this important distinction, by not acknowledging its existence.

I am happy to acknowledge its existence: but I do not think it matters. That it should be thought to matter seems to me to be a symptom of the phenomenon to which I referred at the end of the first Chapter: the obsession that the way we use statements involved in communicating know-how ought somehow to be able to be forced into the same moulds as the statements we make which are involved in communicating know-that. It matters if we tell someone that all swans are white, even if we have the very best of reasons for believing that they are white, for what we have communicated is false. But when it comes to teaching know-how, it matters not at all whether a comparison is true or whether one ought to treat it as if it were true. In either eventuality one ought to behave in the same way.

What I am trying to show is that the procedures one adopts (and ought to adopt) in establishing the truth-value of a comparison (or in establishing what its truth-value ought to be) are the same, whether one is investigating a lofty or an earthy comparison. I am not arguing that these three procedures are necessarily the only procedures one adopts (or ought to adopt) in establishing the truth-value of a comparison. There may be others. All I will hazard is the guess that if there should be another maxim, it would apply alike to lofty and earthy comparisons because they have the same logic.

The Third Maxim leaves unanswered the vexed question of who the experts may be. On very many occasions there is no question about who the experts are. It is perverse to try and be clear about the procedures in the unusual cases until one is clear about the usual procedures.

SUMMARY: The Third Maxim is that when entertaining the idea of using a comparison, one ought to establish its truth or falsehood by taking the word of the experts in the particular pattern of purposive behaviour involved. These are 'received reasons' for thinking a principle to be true or false.

CHAPTER THREE

Universality and Related Matters

1. *Universality*

IN the last Chapter I tried to establish that the truth-values of both lofty and earthy comparisons are established by the same procedures: viz. by use of the Three Maxims. I have now to try and establish that the same principles of inference are employed in the use of both lofty and earthy comparisons. But before doing this there are some gaps in the argument to be filled in.

I use the word 'unconfined' (of weak comparisons) and not the more conventional word 'universal' because it is important to put a limit to the universality of the concepts of 'anyone' (and 'everyone' for that matter) in this context. This is the second place in my argument in which I think I am saying something different from what most philosophers would say. If John Doe says that action A is better than action B in achieving a certain result in certain circumstances for anyone, he is not necessarily affirming that it is better for anyone in the world. Someone who is a citizen of Outer Mongolia may not find it so. He is not necessarily denying that a citizen of Outer Mongolia may find that action A is not better than action B in these circumstances. But this does not affect the usefulness of John Doe's comparison because when he is imparting this knowledge to others, he does not expect those others to include any citizens of Outer Mongolia. Nor would citizens of Outer Mongolia be likely to look to him for advice. Thus for the purposes for which John Doe needs unconfined weak comparisons (among other things for passing knowhow on to other people), he does not need to affirm that unconfined weak comparisons are inane, true or false universally, only that they are inane, true or false for those people who are likely to be exposed to them.

In this context I would like to draw an analogy between the

way in which I think the concept of 'anyone' ought to be used in this context and the concept of a 'population' as used by biologists. To a biologist the concept of a 'population' means roughly any group of individuals who have a modest probability, within any generation, of meeting and mating. Where high improbability takes over, there lies the border of a population.

With unconfined weak comparisons the borderline is analogous: when a spokesman makes an unconfined weak comparison all he asserts is that it is inane, true or false for anyone likely to be exposed to it—but not necessarily so for everyone in the world. (We may notice, in passing, that with the improvement in communications, the class of persons likely to be exposed to some people's comparisons—the President of the U.S.A., for instance—is increasing rapidly.) This fact that when a spokesman makes an unconfined weak comparison he may not necessarily be affirming its truth-value universally seems to me to be a very obvious but nevertheless important point.

That philosophers have worried about the universality of, e.g., moral principles seems to me to be another symptom of the phenomenon to which I referred at the end of the first Chapter: the obsession that the way we use statements involved in communicating know-how ought somehow to be able to be forced into the same moulds as the statements we make which are involved in communicating know-that. For, if someone says that all swans are white, then he is committed to the (false) belief that every single swan the world over is white; whereas if someone says that a Prairie Oyster is a better breakfast than porridge after a drinking bout, he does not commit himself to saying that it is better for every individual person in the world to have a Prairie Oyster rather than porridge for breakfast after a drinking bout. The citizens of Outer Mongolia may (for all he knows) be different.

One should not overemphasise the differences of opinion between spokesmen in the unconfined weak comparisons which they advance on the same patterns of purposive behaviour. Certainly when we are young there is virtual unanimity of opinion among all grown-ups about a host of unconfined weak comparisons, from the very many a child is exposed to in learning how to talk, to comparisons like the Nanny's comparison (Mark II).

I am not denying that the surprises occur, that the arguments take place, and that the philosophical difficulties arise when spokesmen's unconfined weak comparisons are not in agreement. When they are not in agreement, I shall say that they conflict with one another. By a weak comparison which conflicts with the form of Mark II comparison given on p. 24, I mean an unconfined weak comparison of the form: Action A is *not* a better way of performing the pattern of purposive behaviour P than action B if one wants to achieve result R in circumstances (1) and (2); or an unconfined weak comparison of the form: Action **B** is a better way of performing the pattern of purposive behaviour P than action **A** if one wants to achieve result R in circumstances (1) and (2). (That action C may be better than either action A or action B does not concern us at this stage.) But let us not contemplate the embarrassing development that unconfined weak comparisons may conflict with one another until we are clear about their use when there is virtual unanimity about their truth-value.

SUMMARY: If a spokesman says of an unconfined weak comparison that it is inane, true or false, one ought not to conclude that it is so for everyone in the world. The extent of its universality need only embrace the population likely to be exposed to it. Although the more perplexing philosophical difficulties arise when spokesmen's unconfined weak comparisons conflict with one another, there is virtual unanimity of opinion about unconfined weak comparisons over a wide range of patterns of purposive behaviour.

2. *General and Specific Unconfined Weak Comparisons*

I have nothing useful to say about the constituent elements which I have called respectively 'action A', 'comparison', or 'action B' in my form of comparison (Mark II). But there are features in the specification of the circumstances which call for comment.

In colloquial English it is common for the circumstances of a comparison to be assumed because of very generally followed conventions or simply to be taken for granted to save time. There is no magic in specifying *two* circumstances, there may be more than two or none at all. If we revert to the Mark II comparison and modify it slightly, it makes perfectly good sense to say:

COMPARISON (MARK III)

'Action A is a better way of performing the pattern of purposive behaviour P than action B if one wants to achieve result R.'—*Spokesman.*

Once again to give examples.

The Nanny's comparison (Mark III)

Action A:	'Using the pot
Comparison:	is a better way of defecating than
Action B:	using one's pants
Result R:	if one wants to stay clean.'
Spokesman:	—*John Doe.*

The Etymologist's comparison (Mark III)

Action A:	'Calling that stuff "spaghetti"
Comparison:	is a better way of communicating in words than
Action B:	calling it "bascotti"
Result R:	if one wants to be understood by people.'
Spokesman:	—*John Doe.*

And so on through all the original Mark I examples I gave on pages 18–21. But much more caution is needed here. The truth-value of a comparison may change in the move from Mark II to Mark III. Thus, the Dietician's comparison becomes:

Universality and Related Matters

The Dietician's comparison (Mark III)

Action A:	'Swallowing a Prairie Oyster
Comparison:	is a better way of having breakfast than
Action B:	eating porridge
Result R:	if one wants to assuage one's hunger.'
Spokesman:	*—John Doe.*

But although the Dietician's comparison (Mark II) may be true, the Dietician's comparison (Mark III) may be false. Swallowing a Prairie Oyster is (one may surmise) only a better way of having breakfast than eating porridge if one wants to assuage one's hunger *after a drinking bout*. The whole point about Prairie Oysters is that they are for use when one has a hangover.

Similarly with the Mechanic's comparison which becomes:

The Mechanic's comparison (Mark III)

Action A:	'Using the starting handle
Comparison:	is a better way of starting a car than
Action B:	using the self-starter
Result R:	if one wants to avoid damaging the batteries.'
Spokesman:	*—Richard Roe.*

To which someone may retort: 'What on earth do you mean? What is the self-starter there for?' Answer: 'I mean if one wants to avoid damaging the batteries *in cold weather.*'

Specifying the circumstances limits the *generality* of an unconfined weak comparison. Not to specify the circumstances makes the comparison more general. To say that swallowing a Prairie Oyster is a better way of having breakfast than eating porridge is to give a more general guide to action than to say that swallowing a Prarie Oyster is a better way of having breakfast than eating porridge after a drinking bout. The latter is more specific than the former.

Specifying a circumstance both reduces the number of patterns of purposive behaviour to which an unconfined weak comparison is relevant and adds a new factor to the comparison. The truth-

43

value of the more specific comparison cannot be derived from the truth-value of the more general comparison by the principles of inference of traditional logic. For example, one of the principles of inference of traditional logic is the so-called *modus ponendo ponens*: if p, then q; but p; therefore q. If George is John's father, then George is male; but George is John's father; therefore George is male.

If the truth-value of the more specific comparison could be derived from the truth-value of the corresponding more general comparison by the *modus ponendo ponens,* one would validly be able to infer the truth of a Mark II comparison (q) from the truth of the corresponding Mark III comparison (p). But this cannot always be reliably done and a rule of inference which does not *always* work is of no use. Let me give an illustration to show that it does not always work.

Take the following Mark III comparison (p):

Action A:	'Attending a university
Comparison:	is a better way of learning the law than
Action B:	going to a firm of law crammers
Result R:	if one wants to pass one's Bar Finals.'
Spokesman:	*—John Doe.*

Take the corresponding Mark II comparison (q):

Action A:	'Attending a university
Comparison:	is a better way of learning the law than
Action B:	going to a firm of law crammers
Result R:	if one wants to pass one's Bar Finals
Circumstance (1):	in the shortest possible time
Circumstance (2):	with the minimum of expense.'
Spokesman:	*—John Doe.*

If the *modus ponendo ponens* enabled one to establish the truth of q given the truth of b in this context, one would be able to infer the truth of the Mark II from the truth of the Mark III comparison. But a moment's reflection will make clear that one can perfectly consistently hold p (i.e. that attending a university is a better way of learning the law than going to a firm of law crammers if one wants to pass one's Bar Finals) and not q (i.e. that it is false that attending a university is a better way of learning the law than going to a firm of law crammers if one wants to pass one's Bar Finals in the shortest possible time and at minimum expense). The circumstances that one wants to pass in the shortest possible time and at the minimum expense add new factors to the situation which may call for different advice.

Thus we now come to the first of the principles of inference which are (or ought to be) employed in the use of both lofty and earthy comparisons:

> *Principle 1:* A true more specific comparison may not necessarily be validly derivable from the corresponding true more general comparison.

We have seen this principle applying to earthy comparisons (the Law Tutor's). It applies equally to lofty comparisons. It does not follow from the truth of the comparison that telling the truth is a better way of behaving than telling a lie if one wants to preserve the fabric of society, that it is true that telling the truth is a better way of behaving than telling a lie if one wants to preserve the fabric of society when confronting a homicidal maniac in pursuit of his victim.

Not only does the *modus ponendo ponens* sometimes render invalid inferences of specific from more general comparisons, but the *modus tollendo tollens* does not work either in this context. The *modus tollendo tollens* is another of the principles of inference of traditional logic: if p, then q; but not q; therefore not p. If George is John's father, then George is male; but George is not male; therefore George is not John's father. It does not follow from the falsehood of a Mark II comparison (q) that its Mark III counterpart (p) is false. It does not follow from the falsehood of the comparison that attending a university is a better way of learning the law than going to a firm of law crammers if one wants to pass one's Bar Finals in the shortest possible time and at the minimum expense, that it is necessarily false that attending a university is a better way of learning the law than going to a firm of law crammers if one wants to pass one's Bar Finals.

So, the second of the principles of inference which are (or ought to be) employed in the use of both lofty and earthy comparisons:

> *Principle 2:* A false more specific comparison may not necessarily falsify the corresponding true more general comparison.

It does not follow from the falsehood of the comparison that telling the truth is a better way of behaving than telling a lie if one wants to preserve the fabric of society when confronting a homicidal maniac in pursuit of his victim, that it is necessarily false that telling the truth is a better way of behaving than telling a lie if one wants to preserve the fabric of society.

These are by no means the only two valid principles of inference which are (or ought to be) employed in the use of both lofty and earthy comparisons, but they are sufficient at this stage in my argument.

SUMMARY: One may distinguish between Mark II comparisons and more general unconfined weak comparisons (in which few or none of the circumstances are specified). The more general unconfined weak comparison may be shown thus:

COMPARISON (MARK III)

> *'Action A is a better way of performing the pattern of purposive behaviour P than action B if one wants to achieve result R.'—Spokesman.*

A true more specific comparison may not necessarily be validly derivable from the corresponding true more general comparison. A false more specific comparison may not necessarily falsify the corresponding true more general comparison.

46

3. *Complete and Incomplete Unconfined Weak Comparisons*

As we saw, a performance of a pattern of purposive behaviour is usually (and ought to be) compared by someone with another performance of the same pattern, on its success in achieving the result at which the pattern of purposive behaviour is aimed. This has led some philosophers (e.g. Aaron Sloman, who calls what I call 'the result R' the 'basis' of a comparison) to insist that every comparison *must* have a result. But to legislate thus severely obscures the way in which we actually use our language. It rules out of court comparisons we often make.

The fact is that the result R is the one constituent element in a comparison which, in colloquial speech, we are most likely to assume, or to take for granted, or leave vague by accident or design.

If we revert to the Mark III comparison and modify it slightly, it makes perfectly good sense to say:

COMPARISON (MARK IV)

'Action A is a better way of performing the pattern of purposive behaviour P than action B.'—*Spokesman.*

To mark the difference between the unconfined weak comparisons which we have so far been considering in which the result R is specified (albeit so nebulously as to render the comparison inane) and an unconfined weak comparison in which the result is not specified, I will call the former 'complete' and the latter 'incomplete'. Thus anyone who affirms that action A is a better way of doing something than action B without specifying the result is making an incomplete unconfined weak comparison. An incomplete unconfined weak comparison can (theoretically) always be transformed into a complete comparison by specifying the result, except (as we shall see) in the important case of moral principles.

Once again I will give examples, but allowing myself more

flexibility. Nothing very much hinges on how Mark IV comparisons are expressed; and where a relevant circumstance has disappeared in the passage from Mark II to III, I have re-introduced it in Mark IV in order that I may be able to discuss the associated comparisons later in my argument.

The Nanny's comparison (Mark IV)
Action A: 'Using the pot
Comparison: is a better way of defecating than
Action B: using one's pants.'
Spokesman: —*John Doe.*

The Etymologist's comparison (Mark IV)
Action A: 'Calling that stuff "spaghetti"
Comparison: is a better way of communicating in
              words than
Action B: calling it "bascotti".'
Spokesman: —*Richard Roe.*

The Mechanic's comparison (Mark IV)
Action A: 'In cold weather, using the starting handle
Comparison: is a better way of starting a car than
Action B: using the self-starter.'
Spokesman: —*John Doe.*

The Dietician's comparison (Mark IV)
Action A: 'With a hang-over, swallowing a
              Prairie Oyster
Comparison: is a better way of having breakfast than
Action B: eating porridge.'
Spokesman: —*Richard Roe.*

The Law Tutor's comparison (Mark IV)
Action A: 'Going to a firm of law crammers
Comparison: is a better way of learning the law quickly
              than
Action B: attending a university.'
Spokesman: —*John Doe.*

The Logical Positivist's comparison (Mark IV)

Action A:	'Avoiding the predicates "true" or "false" of statements other than tautologies and scientific hypotheses
Comparison:	is a better way of arguing than
Action B:	predicating truth or falsehood of such statements.'
Spokesman:	—Richard Roe.

The Probation Officer's comparison (Mark IV)

Action A:	'Drinking a glass of whisky
Comparison:	is a better thing to do than
Action B:	taking drugs.'
Spokesman:	—John Doe.

The Musicologist's comparison (Mark IV)

Action A:	'Playing on a harpsichord
Comparison:	is a better way of performing any of Bach's forty-eight Preludes and Fugues than
Action B:	playing on a piano.'
Spokesman:	—Richard Roe.

The Businessman's comparison (Mark IV)

Action A:	'Speaking the whole truth
Comparison:	is a better way of behaving than
Action B:	concealing a relevant fact.'
Spokesman:	—John Doe.

The Aesthetician's comparison (Mark IV)

Action A:	'Wearing a tie of any colour other than magenta
Comparison:	is a better way of dressing than
Action B:	wearing a magenta tie with a pink shirt.'
Spokesman:	—Richard Roe.

The point to notice here about the unconfined weak comparisons listed above is that they function perfectly well in our language whether they are complete or incomplete: they give us effective guidance on what to do. As a necessary ingredient in communicating know-how from one person to another, the result R in an unconfined weak comparison is otiose. But there is an important sense in which the truth-value of a comparison may be dependent on the result R. The Dietician's comparison may be true if the result at which the pattern of purposive behaviour is aimed is to assuage one's hunger, but false if the result aimed at is to stop one drinking ever again. The Law Tutor's comparison may be true if the result aimed at is to pass one's Bar Finals in the shortest time, but false if the result aimed at is to make one's mark as an academic lawyer. The Businessman's comparison may be true if the object of the exercise is to get a loan from a banker, but false if the object is to keep out of jail. And so on.

It may very well be that it is *better* to specify the result of an unconfined comparison *than to* leave the result vague if one wants to communicate with precision—but that in itself is an unconfined weak comparison (and another matter). Of course it is true that when defending a comparison or giving reasons for a comparison, then, to any intelligent critic, the result R (or basis or whatever) will be one of the crucial factors in the explanation. But to concede this much is not to admit that a comparison must (logically must) have a basis.

SUMMARY: One may distinguish between more general forms of unconfined weak comparisons which are 'complete' (as, for instance, the Mark III examples), and those in which the result R is assumed, or taken for granted, or left vague by accident or design. These will be called 'incomplete' and may be shown thus:

COMPARISON (MARK IV)

'Action A is a better way of performing the pattern of purposive behaviour P than action B.'

The truth-value of a comparison may be dependent upon what the result aimed at is; but an incomplete unconfined weak comparison functions perfectly efficiently in our language.

CHAPTER FOUR

Strong Comparisons

1. *Comparisons (Mark V)*

IN II.1 I defined a comparison which conflicts with a Mark II comparison as a comparison of the form: Action A is *not* a better way of performing the pattern of purposive behaviour P than action B if one wants to achieve result R in circumstances (1) and (2); or a comparison of the form: Action **B** is a better way of performing the pattern of purposive behaviour P than action A if one wants to achieve result R in circumstances (1) and (2). That action C may be a better way than either action A or action B, I wrote, did not then concern us. It does concern us now because of mankind's continuous search for *the best* way of accomplishing the tasks, producing the results, reaching the goals, pursuing the ends and achieving the ambitions we set ourselves in life. Thus we come to make strong comparisons:

COMPARISON (MARK V)

'Action C is the best way of performing the pattern of purposive behaviour P.'—*Spokesman.*

This as it stands is an incomplete form of comparison, but it can be completed by specifying the result: 'if one wants to achieve result R'.

It is clear that, but for one complication, a Mark V comparison can be analysed out in terms of Mark IV comparisons. Or, to put it another way, Mark V comparisons can be constructed from Mark IV comparisons and no other forms of statement. For a Mark V comparison is true if, but only if, action C is better than all other *possible* actions A, B, D, E, F and so on.*

* 'The superlative raises no special problems, being in principle superfluous.' (Quine: *Philosophy of Logic*, p. 78.)

The complication arises from the need to put some kind of finite limit on the class of all other possible actions, because clearly no one would be able to state that action C is the best way to go about some pattern of purposive behaviour if he had to spend the rest of his life comparing it with other possible ways of going about the job—as Moore pointed out very many years ago. [10]

So in practice, a spokesman feels himself justified (and ought to feel himself justified) in saying that action C is the best way to go about a pattern of purposive behaviour if it is better than any other action *of which he is apprised*. (What I mean by 'apprised' in this context I try to make clearer in the next section.) Thus:

The Dietician's comparison (Mark V)

Action C: 'With a hang-over, swallowing a Prairie Oyster
Comparison: is the best way of having breakfast.'
Spokesman: —*John Doe.*

This comparison will be true if, but only if, swallowing a Prairie Oyster is better than having a marine's breakfast (an aspirin and a cigarette), drinking coffee or Alka Seltzer, eating porridge, taking a hair of the dog that bit one, or any other way of having breakfast of which the spokesman is apprised. And so on with the other comparisons.

So we get the other comparisons (not *all* of which translate very readily into a strong form of comparison for a reason we will come to later):

The Nanny's comparison (Mark V)

Comparison: 'It is best
Action C: to use the pot.'
Spokesman: —*Richard Roe.*

The Etymologist's comparison (Mark V)

Comparison: 'It is best
Action C: to describe that stuff as "spaghetti".'
Spokesman: —*John Doe.*

Strong Comparisons

The Mechanic's comparison (Mark V)

Comparison: 'In cold weather it is best
Action C: to start one's car by using the starting
                handle.'
Spokesman: —Richard Roe.

The Law Tutor's comparison (Mark V)

Comparison: 'It is best
Action C: to go to a law crammer to pass one's Bar
                Finals in the shortest possible time.'
Spokesman: —John Doe.

The Logical Positivist's comparison (Mark V)

Comparison: 'It is best
Action C: not to predicate truth or falsehood of
                statements other than tautologies and
                scientific hypotheses.'
Spokesman: —Richard Roe.

The Musicologist's comparison (Mark V)

Comparison: 'It is best to
Action C: play Bach's forty-eight Preludes and
                Fugues on the harpsichord.'
Spokesman: —John Doe.

The Aesthetician's comparison (Mark V)

Comparison: 'It is best
Action C: not to wear a pink tie with a magenta
                shirt.'
Spokesman: —Richard Roe.

Nothing very much hinges on the exact way in which these are phrased. These unconfined strong comparisons are typically used where something has to be done (or not done) and precision in the expression of them is not important. They are to be found in what others have called by an astonishing variety of names: precepts, hints, tips, attitudes, policies, maxims, proverbs, imperatives, conventions, recommendations, opinions and many others.

The importance of the Mark V examples is also manifest in the explanation of another posit which has always troubled moral philosophers: the word 'ought'. In English, that one ought always to perform a pattern of purposive behaviour in the best way, is true *by definition*. 'With a hang-over, swallowing a Prairie Oyster is the best way of having breakfast.'='One ought to swallow a Prairie Oyster for breakfast if one has a hang-over.' 'It is best to describe that stuff as "spaghetti".'='One ought to call that stuff "spaghetti".' 'It is best not to predicate truth or falsehood of statements other than tautologies and scientific hypotheses.'='One ought not to predicate truth or falsehood of statements other than tautologies and scientific hypotheses.' These are necessary truths because they express our determination to use symbols in a certain way. Thus:

'Action C is the best way of performing the pattern of = purposive behaviour P.'   'When performing the pattern of purposive behaviour P, one ought to do C.'
—*Spokesman*.

The incomplete strong comparison can be completed by specifying the result.

We can thus remove the mystery from the troublesome word 'ought'. And with only a touch of legerdemain we can do the same for the words 'good', 'bad', 'right', and 'wrong'. Notice that it is not necessarily good to do action A, if action A is better than action B, because they may both be indifferent ways of going about performing the pattern of purposive behaviour P. It was for this reason that some of the old Mark IV examples did not translate very readily into Mark V examples. It is not necessarily good to drink a glass of whisky simply because it is better to drink a glass of whisky than to take drugs if you want to induce euphoria.

But it is (by definition) 'good' to do what one ought to do, and 'bad' to do what one ought not to do. Similarly, it is 'right' to do what one ought to do, and 'wrong' to do what one ought not to do. So the troublesome words 'good', 'right', 'bad' and 'wrong' *in this context* (i.e. when it comes to evaluating *actions*) can be analysed in terms of 'ought' and 'ought not', which, in turn, can be disposed of in terms of 'better than'.

A critic may argue that it is false to say 'C is the best way of doing P' entails that one ought to do C to achieve P, for if one ought to do C presumably one ought not to perform any alternative in lieu of C. But one might hold, for example, that the best way to make coffee is C, but that B is a perfectly acceptable method. In these circumstances one would not say that one ought to do B in lieu of C.

My answer is that the critic does not take his coffee-making seriously enough. As far as the experts are concerned nothing is 'acceptable' but the very best. It might be that C is not a better way of achieving P than B—in that they are both equally good. But if C is a better way of making coffee than B *and one is serious,* then one ought to do C.

SUMMARY: What I shall call a 'strong comparison':

COMPARISON (MARK V)

'*Action C is the best way of performing the pattern of purposive behaviour P.'—Spokesman.*

is incomplete as it stands but can be completed by specifying the result R at which the pattern of purposive behaviour in question is aimed. A Mark V comparison is true if, but only if, action C is better than any other action of which the spokesman is apprised. In English, that one ought always to perform a pattern of purposive behaviour in the best way, is true by definition. 'Good', 'bad', 'right' and 'wrong' can be defined in terms of 'ought' and 'ought not'.

2. *The Field of the Spokesman's Acquaintance*

In having breakfast, starting a car, inducing euphoria, etc., there is no *logical* reason why the *only* performances of which John Doe is apprised should not be his own performances of the pattern of purposive behaviour in question. If this is so, the 'other actions of which he is apprised'—let us call this his 'field of acquaintance' —is limited to his own performances and any innovations to his own performances which his imaginative insight can conjure up. But in practice, John Doe does not have to rely upon his own resources because he has other people's knowledge and experience available to him.

It is highly improbable that John Doe would, through his own imaginative insight, stumble upon the possibility of having a Prairie Oyster for breakfast when he has a hang-over—although, once upon a time, someone undoubtedly invented Prairie Oysters. What happened in John Doe's case was probably something like this. One morning, after a drinking bout, as he flinched at the thought of eating porridge, or drinking some orange juice, or smoking a cigarette, Richard Roe appeared and said: 'What you need is a Prairie Oyster', or 'A Prairie Oyster is the best breakfast when you have a hang-over', or 'What you ought to have is a Prairie Oyster', or 'Why don't you try a Prairie Oyster?' Richard Roe proceeded to fix him one and thereupon John Doe's field of acquaintance was informed and extended by Richard Roe's experience. Put another way: Richard Roe had imparted some knowledge to John Doe.

The vogue of the Logical Positivist's comparison can be explained in very similar terms. Philosophers had been bemused for centuries on whether certain 'metaphysical' statements could be said to be true or false. Along came a group of gentlemen from Vienna who said (roughly): 'But these sentences are literally meaningless', or 'These sentences can be neither true nor false because they cannot be verified', or 'One ought not to predicate truth or falsehood of statements other than tautologies and scientific hypotheses'. Let no one doubt now that, at that time, this discovery was a great break-through.

With other patterns of purposive behaviour, other people's experiences may be the *only* experience which John Doe has in his field of acquaintance other than what his own imaginative insight can supply. In learning to speak a language, a child is utterly dependent on other people's know-how. Again, in any individual's lifetime it is unlikely that he will need to serve his articles or pass his professional examinations more than once. So in purposive behaviour directed towards this end of becoming a qualified professional man, unless he is to rely entirely upon his own imaginative insight, John Doe must draw heavily upon other people's experience in achieving his aim.

So the 'field of his acquaintance' is very rarely limited to a spokesman's own experience and imaginative insight. It will almost always also embrace knowledge he has picked up from other people in his population, which will include knowledge which they, in their turn, have picked up from others. When I talk of the field known to the spokesman, I mean to embrace the spokesman's own experience and the experiences which they have communicated to him of those from whom he has learnt.

It is when patterns of purposive behaviour are imparted from one person to another that (what I will call) 'situations of apprenticeship' occur. There is a situation of apprenticeship (in my sense) when anyone is teaching anyone, or learning from anyone, what to *do,* as when John Doe learns about Prairie Oysters from Richard Roe. Thus there is a situation of apprenticeship where any beginner learns from an expert, when someone sets a fashion, where a disciple follows a prophet, where a trend-setter influences his audience, where a master imparts his skill to a pupil, but (above all) where a child is brought up by its parents. (Moreover, we are all, throughout our lives, in a situation of apprenticeship about how we ought to use words—and from a philosopher's point of view this is, perhaps, the most important of the lot.)

There are less easily recognisable situations of apprenticeship—in which John Doe may not be in need of guidance (in the sense of *asking* for help), but may nevertheless behave differently as a result of picking up another way of performing a pattern of purposive behaviour from someone else. Thus, in the field of social etiquette many people were influenced in the 1950's by Nancy Mitford's proclamations of what was U and what was non-U in their choice of words. They found themselves hesitating before they spoke of the 'mantel-piece' although they would have indignantly denied needing guidance in this field. The truth is that 'trend-setters' influence people over fields of behaviour in which those people may not consciously be seeking advice at all. Contrariwise, some efforts to influence people's behaviour may be counter-productive, as when (it is said) Bertrand Russell took to drinking alcohol during the 1914–18 War because George V had signed the pledge.

Whether a piece of music haunts my mind depends partly on how often I have heard it played; which, in turn, may depend (surprisingly) on whether Desmond Shawe-Taylor admires it and has written so in a newspaper article that I have read. This article may have caused me to buy a recording of the piece of music in question. Thus Desmond Shawe-Taylor, without my ever having met him and without my consciously *seeking* his advice, has influenced my life and caused me to behave differently from the way I would have behaved had I not read his article. I am in a relation of apprenticeship to him.

He may be only one of a number of music critics whose judgments I take seriously. Further, I am only one among many people who are influenced by Shawe-Taylor's criticism. Moreover, it is conceivable (although blessedly unlikely) that some people may be influenced by my taste in music (in which I am no expert) —in the way that I hope to influence some people by my comparisons in fields in which I am an expert. The importance of some works of philosophy may be noticed by the fact that philosophers talk and write differently after having read them. They stop talking (for a year or two while the fashion lasts) about 'analysing' an expression and talk about 'unpacking' its meaning. They stop asking for the 'meaning' of a word and ask for its 'use'. They stop predicating truth or falsehood of statements other than tautologies and scientific hypotheses, and call everything else nonsense. They stop proffering evidence to verify scientific hypotheses and instead offer contrary evidence to falsify scientific hypotheses. And so on.

Our children are peculiarly exposed to their parents' views on a whole range of subjects on which their parents have no sort of title to be considered experts or even good enough to proffer advice at all, in the ordinary course of events. Not only do children learn to speak under the influence of their parents' criticism; but until they are quite old, a parent's slightest wish has prescriptive force for his offspring, even if it is counter-productive in effect. This is because children are inevitably in a relation of apprenticeship to their parents; and this invests their parents' words with an importance it is difficult for others to match.

We read books and newspapers, and watch television and are continuously bombarded with advice, overt and covert, on how we ought to behave. Every public figure tries (somehow or other) to make his little mark on his population and persuade us (at the very least) to vote for him. So much so that one weekly newspaper currently thinks it worth while to put the following advertisement in the London Underground trains:

'Nbdy. fnds. ckry. hnts. in Dltns. wkly.'*

Thus the 'other actions of which he is apprised' can be as perplexing to the spokesman as his visual sensations are to the once blind man who is given the modern operation which enables him to see for the first time. So in deciding how to behave we must pick and choose comparisons, seek and impose order, and devise and test comparisons about what we ought to do. And we do this with the help of *words,* throughout our lives.

SUMMARY: A spokesman's field of acquaintance is rarely limited to his own experience and insight; he has other people's (notably his parents') knowledge available to him.

* What one finds are classified ads.: i.e. know-that, not know-how.

3. *The Drive for Truth and Generality*

Until now I have been shielding my argument from the phenomenon which causes most of the bother. Although nearly everyone would agree that the Nanny's comparison (Mark V) was true, opinions might differ about the Mechanic's comparison and the Law Tutor's comparison (Mark V), and most philosophers would now agree that the Logical Positivist's comparison (Mark V) was false. Embarrassingly enough, comparisons *conflict* with one another. It is an embarrassment because unresolved conflicts of comparisons make the process of imparting knowledge, of instruction and learning, so difficult as to be almost impossible. This is a fact of the utmost importance. Were it not for this fact, there would be no need of the concept of a 'principle'—because a Mark V comparison would be a sufficiently strong posit to do the whole job.

If a child is shown a certain substance and told by one parent that one ought to call it 'bascotti', but is then told by its other parent that it is wrong to call it 'bascotti', it ought to be called 'spaghetti'; if the child then goes back to the first parent who says that it is wrong to call it 'spaghetti', it ought to be called 'bascotti', then that child will not know what it ought to be called. Later in its upbringing it is a matter of considerable importance (as child psychologists never tire of affirming) that each parent's comparisons on matters where a child has a choice should (more often than not) coincide. Where they disagree, they must spend a lot of time explaining *why* they disagree.

Any teacher will appreciate the difficulty of teaching people patterns of purposive behaviour, if his pupils are contemporaneously being fed with conflicting comparisons by rival experts. Some teachers (Mr. and Mrs. Leavis, for example) can get very worked up on this matter. A very important part of a sophisticated education consists in learning how to choose between conflicting advice. We all develop ways and means of doing this. But the important point to grasp is that imparting know-how is virtually impossible if comparisons *always* conflict and there is no means of choosing between them.

This is the drive behind our search for *true* comparisons. Our search for the truth in the case of scientific hypotheses may be motivated by a desire to make reliable predictions about the way things will happen. Our search for true comparisons does not (in this sense) yield any information about the world. But in the absence of any sort of agreement about comparisons, it is impossible for people to impart a certain sort of knowledge to others. Instruction is obstructed unless and until conflict can be resolved. There *need* not be anything more to the truth-value of unconfined comparisons than the urgency of this drive. This is the third thing I have written which is (I think) different from what most other philosophers would say.

Only hermits (from God) and Jesuit novices take instruction in performing patterns of purposive behaviour from one instructor only: everyone else is open to influence from all over the place. There is therefore a need to develop a (dirty word) 'consensus' among spokesmen about what are the best performances of different patterns of purposive behaviour, on how we ought to behave, so that instructors can teach without contradicting one another and pupils can learn effectively and efficiently. It is this which leads to the formulation of 'principles'—the concept which is the central subject of this book.

The use of a comparison in situations where it functions in the teaching-learning process leads to another phenomenon which has potentially dangerous consequences—the tendency to formulate comparisons in a way which is *more general* than the situation warrants. By this I mean that an instructor tends to ignore the special circumstances in his formulation of a comparison in the hope that the circumstances do not matter and the rule can be followed when the circumstances are different.

There is nothing to be criticised in this tendency insofar as it is done to facilitate teaching, by economising in the number of distinctions the pupil has to make. The potentially dangerous consequence lies in supposing that a more general formulation somehow 'covers' situations in which there are special circumstances. This last is a logical howler, because it conflicts with Principle I in the use of comparisons.

SUMMARY: The urge to reach agreement in one's unconfined comparisons springs from a desire to be able to teach and learn efficiently. This same desire produces a tendency to generalise comparisons which may not be justified.

4. *Schools of Thought*

It is a contingent fact that there is at least one (and often more) 'school(s) of thought' about what are better or the best performances of *any* pattern of purposive behaviour. I mean by a school of thought no more than an analogous posit to a biologist's population: a group of people all of whom make more or less the same comparisons about performances of a pattern of purposive behaviour to facilitate the teaching-learning process. People are born in different environments and taught in different ways: the astonishing thing is that there are so comparatively few different schools of thought about the same patterns of purposive behaviour.

But there are differences. Englishmen belong (more or less) to the same school of thought in the language they teach their children. Germans belong to another school of thought, Russians another. In pot training many English parents belong to the same school of thought as many Russian and German parents. In musical aesthetics there tend, usually, to be at least two schools of thought in each language culture: one, 'highbrow'; the other, 'lowbrow'.

The posit of a school of thought is needed in my argument for this reason. There is an important sense in which a school of thought is different from the sum of the people who are members of the school at any one time: for example, the comparisons made by members of the school of thought may be reaffirmed by their pupils after all the original members of the school of thought are dead. We talk, in this context, of a 'tradition'. Schools of thought are usually identifiable by their continual striving to vindicate their own (often false) belief that their own comparisons are better than those of any other school.

A trivial instance of differing schools of thought is to be found, once again, in the business of assuaging one's hunger after a night's sleep. In Spain, a majority of the male inhabitants will breakfast early by drinking a hefty slug of brandy, and will have nothing to eat until ten o'clock or so in the morning. In France, the dominant school of thought judges that the best breakfast is made by drinking a cup of coffee and eating some bread and jam. In England, many feel that they haven't started the day properly unless they have a plate of eggs and bacon under their belts. But the comparisons which produce this different behaviour are not simply the comparisons of a majority of the present generation of breakfast-eaters. They are the result of a store of know-how of that particular pattern of purposive behaviour which has been accumulating after millions of performances over many years by many hundreds and thousands of different people.

Moreover the comparisons of a school of thought may change (sometimes imperceptibly) over the years. Two hundred years ago, if William Cobbett is to be believed, many people in England considered the best breakfast to be a pint of beer and some cold meat. Even people who maintain that comparisons about matters pertaining to 'faith' and 'morals' are 'eternal' and do not change can sometimes be persuaded to agree that these truths have been differently interpreted over the years—and this admission is all one needs.

To try and make my argument more precise: I will talk of a school of thought in a pattern of purposive behaviour where a number of individuals habitually perform that pattern, have learned their know-how from some of the same instructors, and are anxious that their comparisons should tally with one another's so that their knowledge of that pattern of purposive behaviour can be more efficiently imparted to others.

We are now in a position to do a bit more to clear up the

vagueness I acknowledged when I said of a comparison that it was 'unconfined'. All that is needed of a comparison used in a school of thought is that its truth-value should be constant for all adherents of that school and for all their pupils. Since anyone might become a pupil's pupil, there is no logical limit to the class; but where a high degree of improbability lies, there lies the boundary of that school of thought.

SUMMARY: One ought to acknowledge the existence of and the reasons for different schools of thought in performing a pattern of purposive behaviour. Schools of thought spring up to further the efficiency of imparting knowledge from one person to another.

5. Principles

I am now in a position to gather up some of the loose strands in what I have so far argued in order to outline the concept which is the subject matter of this book. An important feature of an unconfined comparison used in a situation of apprenticeship is that, in many contexts, the instructor is coaching his pupil (and that pupil is learning) not only as individuals but as adherents to a school of thought. One of the purposes of the school of thought is to make an attempt to see that comparisons used in imparting knowledge do not conflict with one another more than is unavoidable so that people can acquire knowledge without being confused. Moreover, instructors are not only coaching their pupils at first hand, but in the knowledge that one day these comparisons will be used by their pupils themselves, when these pupils come to instruct others.

Until this stage I have always specified the spokesman who makes the comparison in the examples of comparisons I have given: John Doe or Richard Roe. The progress of the comparison from a confined weak comparison (Mark I), to an unconfined weak comparison (Mark II), to a more general unconfined weak comparison (Mark III), to an incomplete unconfined weak comparison (Mark IV), to an unconfined strong comparison (Mark V), has at each stage been supported by the affirmation of a spokesman—whoever that spokesman may be.

Now we are at the end of the line: the spokesman need not be specified because the spokesman is the school of thought. Having decided what pattern of purposive behaviour is being imparted a principle is *what ought to be taught*—irrespective of whom the individual spokesman may be. It ought to be taught *not* because it is somehow better than what an individual instructor may have to offer (although it will be the best comparison of which he is appraised), but because unless there is some sort of agreement on how it ought to be taught, achievement in teaching and learning is frustrated.

This is the unusual posit I have called a principle. A principle involves us in a unique way which a Mark V comparison does not. If we are adherents to the school of thought of which it forms part, then not only ought we to behave in conformity with it, but we ought to teach it to others as well. The examples we have previously discussed may be expressed as principles in the following ways:

The Nanny's principle: One ought not to mess one's pants.

The Etymologist's principle: One ought to call that stuff 'spaghetti', not 'bascotti';

The Dietician's principle: With a hang-over one ought to breakfast off a Prairie Oyster;

The Mechanic's principle: In cold weather, one ought to start a car with the starting handle, and not the self-starter;

The Law Tutor's principle: To pass one's Bar Finals in the shortest time, one ought to go to a law crammer;

The Logical Positivist's principle: One ought not to predicate truth or falsehood of statements other than tautologies and scientific hypotheses;

The Probation Officer's principle: One ought to drink whisky rather than take drugs;

The Musicologist's principle: To please a German audience, one ought to play the 'forty-eight' on a harpsichord;

The Businessman's principle: One ought to tell the whole truth to one's banker;

The Aestetician's principle: One ought not to wear a pink tie with a magenta shirt.

I shall say of these principles that they are 'complete' if they specify the result at which they are aimed (like the Musicologist's principle) and 'incomplete' if they do not. Each of the others can be made complete by specifying the result at which it is aimed.

What I have tried to do is to cut the concept of a principle down to a manageable size. When someone says of a principle that it is true, he is saying that this is an unconfined strong comparison which is or ought to be taught by and to adherents of his school of thought in situations of apprenticeship. Its truth-value is independent of him or any other instructor, for it produces the results at which the pattern of purposive behaviour is aimed. There are ways, therefore, in which it is an 'objective fact'. But there are others in which it may be a 'matter of opinion'. We cannot do without principles because as members of a school of thought they are a verbal means by which we transmit know-how to beginners in any pattern of purposive behaviour.

If a principle is concerned with a pattern of purposive behaviour which we will never be called upon to perform, we look on with amused amazement at the passions which seem to be aroused by decisions where principles conflict. But not so when it does concern us. And there is one sort of principle which concerns everyone the world over: those which concern the pattern of purposive behaviour (if we acknowledge that there is such a pattern) involved in how we ought to live as human beings.

SUMMARY: 'Principles' ought to be looked upon as unconfined strong comparisons in which the spokesman has been supplanted by the 'school of thought'. Principles are 'complete' when they specify the result at which they are aimed, 'incomplete' when they do not.

CHAPTER FIVE

Principles

1. *Moral Principles*

So far I have contented myself with differentiating between what I have called 'earthy' and 'lofty' comparisons. I must now introduce the concept of 'moral' in this context, so that moral principles can be examined alongside other principles. (I take it that it is obvious that a moral principle is a species of lofty, rather than earthy, comparison.) Here I am in something of a difficulty because I argue later that there is no inconsistency in a person holding that there are *no* moral principles. It is sometimes (mistakenly) argued that if a person holds the position that there are no moral principles, then he ought to act just as he pleases: one of the purposes of my argument is to show that this does *not* follow at all. What I can do is to indicate a principle which, if someone concedes that there is such a thing as a moral principle, would be agreed by such a person to be a *moral* principle. I will, quite arbitrarily, take the principles that one ought not to say what is false, and that one ought not to kill other human beings, as paradigms of what people, who believe that there *are* moral principles, mean by the expression.

My argument is that moral principles have the same logic as the ten principles listed in the previous Chapter. For, to reiterate at the risk of being tiresome, two statements may be said to have the same logic if (a) their truth-values are established by the same procedures, and (b) the same principles of inference are employed in the use of the two. My argument is, in brief, that the truth-values of the ten principles listed in the previous Chapter are established by the same procedures as the two moral principles just given, and the same principles of inference are employed in the use of the two different kinds of principle.

Principles, I have argued, are a variety of comparison. The

truth-value of a comparison is established by the procedures outlined in Chapter Two, summarised in the Three Maxims. So both the principles, that with a hang-over one ought to breakfast off a Prairie Oyster, and the principle that one ought not to say what is false, would be assumed to be inane unless they could be established to be true or false. The First Maxim is more a declaration of intent than a procedure; the Second Maxim, however, is to the point. When advancing the two, one sets out to show (and ought to set out to show) that the *consequences* of adopting them both would conduce to the result at which the particular pattern of purposive behaviour in question is aimed.

This, indeed, is what we do, both in the case of moral and other principles. We are taught in childhood of the happy consequences which attended Abraham Lincoln's refusal to tell lies and of the unfortunate consequences which befell the shepherd-boy who called, 'Wolf! Wolf!', once too often. One would similarly advocate acceptance of the Dietician's principle by giving teleological reasons in justification of it: that swallowing a Prairie Oyster was more likely to assuage hunger than any other breakfast anyone could eat. It would not be difficult to produce instances of the teleological reasons one could adduce for all the other principles listed in the previous Chapter, but I will not try the reader's patience that far. The teleological reasons in favour of the principle that one ought not to kill other human beings are too well known to bear repetition.

By the Third Maxim, when entertaining the idea of using the Dietician's principle or of using the no-falsehoods principle, one would establish their truth or falsehood in one's own mind by a consideration of the advice of the experts on the particular pattern of purposive behaviour involved. What medical practitioners say about the Dietician's principle is of crucial importance; as is what Socrates or the Church teaches of the no-falsehoods principle. So I argue that the truth-values of moral principles are established by the same procedures as other principles. We have now to identify the principles of inference which are employed in the use of moral principles and others.

It will be recalled that when outlining the principles of inference which are employed in the use of both lofty and earthy comparisons, I argued that there were at least two such principles:

Principle 1: A true more specific comparison may not necessarily be derivable from the corresponding true more general comparison;

Principle 2: A false more specific comparison may not necessarily falsify the corresponding true more general comparison.

How do these principles of inference work out when they are applied to principles themselves?

I pointed out in II.2 that it does not follow from the truth of the Mark III comparison that attending a university is a better way of learning the law than going to a firm of law crammers if one wants to pass one's Bar Finals, that the corresponding Mark II comparison is true—that attending a university is a better way of learning the law than going to a firm of law crammers if one wants to pass one's Bar Finals in the shortest possible time and at the minimum expense.

Consider this move in relation to principles: from the general principle that to pass one's Bar Finals one ought to attend a university, to the more specific principle that to pass one's Bar Finals in the shortest possible time and with minimum expense one ought to attend a university. Or from the general principle that to please a German audience, one ought to play the 'forty-eight' on a harpsichord, to the more specific principle that to please a German audience in a small hall one ought to play the 'forty-eight' on a harpsichord. This move does not work.

There is no inconsistency in holding that it is true that to pass one's Bar Finals one ought to attend a university, and in holding (at the same time) that it is false that to pass one's Bar Finals in the shortest possible time and with minimum expense one ought to attend a university (because, e.g., to pass one's Bar Finals in the shortest possible time and with minimum expense one ought to go to a firm of law crammers). Similarly, there is no inconsistency in holding that it is true that to please a German audience one ought to play the 'forty-eight' on a harpsichord, and in holding that it is false that to please a German audience in a small hall one ought to play the 'forty-eight' on a harpsichord (because, e.g., in a small hall the quality of sound produced by a harpsichord jars).

Similarly with moral principles. One may not validly infer from the principle that one ought not to kill other human beings that one ought not to kill convicted murderers or one's enemies in battle. It is perfectly consistent to hold both that one ought not to kill other human beings and to hold that one ought to hang murderers. (Convinced Abolitionists may question the consistency of the latter position; but most would disagree with them.) Again, it is perfectly consistent to hold both that it is true that one ought not to say what is false, and that it is false that one ought not to say what is false to the alcoholic looking for whisky, or the homicidal maniac looking for his victim, or the heroin-addict looking for his supplies.

So much for Principle 1. The same applies to Principle 2. It does not follow from the falsehood of the principle that to pass one's Bar Finals in the shortest possible time and with minimum expense one ought to attend a university, that it is necessarily false that to pass one's Bar Finals one ought to attend a university. It does not follow from the falsehood of the principle that one ought not to say what is false to the homicidal maniac looking for his victim, that it is necessarily false that one ought not to say what is false.

So I would argue that Principles 1 and 2 apply alike to moral principles and others.

Are there other principles of inference one employs (and ought to employ) in using principles? It may be worth listing three, although they may appear so trivial as to be barely worth mentioning.

Principle 3: One may validly derive from any unconfined comparison (whether moral or not) the corresponding comparison confined to a specific individual.

From the Musicologist's principle, John Doe may validly infer that, to please a German audience, *he* ought to play the 'forty-eight' on a harpsichord. From the no-falsehoods principle, Richard Roe can validly infer that *he* ought not to say what is false. And so on.

Principle 4: One may validly derive from a strong comparison the corresponding weak comparison.

From the principle that one ought not to say what is false it follows that it is better not to say what is false than to tell a falsehood. From the principle that one ought not to wear a pink tie with a magenta shirt, it follows that it is better not to wear a pink tie with a magenta shirt, than to wear a pink tie in these circumstances. And so on. It is (perhaps) worth reiterating the obvious truth that the reverse does not hold. From the comparison that it is better to drink whisky than to take drugs to induce euphoria, it does not follow that one ought to drink whisky.

Principle 5: One may validly derive a comparison from the corresponding comparison expressed in the negative.

It follows from the Musicologist's principle that to please a German audience one ought *not* to play the 'forty-eight' on anything other than a harpsichord. It follows from the no-falsehood principle that one ought to speak the truth. There are some fine distinctions to be made here (which I shall not attempt to work out) on whether the corresponding negative is *exactly* equivalent. With a little touching up they can be made to be exactly equivalent.

There may well be other principles of inference in the use of principles and other comparisons which I have not thought of. My contention is only that these principles of inference (whatever they may be) are the same whether one is applying them to earthy comparisons (like the Nanny's) or whether one is applying them to the loftiest moral principles. They all have the same logic.

SUMMARY: Moral principles and others have the same logic.

2. *Second-Order Comparisons*

I have argued that the drive for the truth in principles springs from a realisation that conflicting principles lead to inefficiency in the teaching-learning process. I come now to one of the more difficult features of my argument. What ought one to do when true principles conflict? It is certainly the case that one ought not to hurt other people's feelings, and it is also certainly the case that one ought to tell the truth. What ought one to do when some atrocious amateur performer of any pattern of purposive behaviour asks one what one thinks of his performance? As a child at an old-fashioned school, a pupil was taught that it was true that one ought to avoid punishment, but also that one ought to tell the truth. Sometimes, as when someone had inadvertently broken a window with a cricket ball, these two true principles were in conflict.

The resolution of a conflict of this sort will often take the form of another comparison: principle A is *more important than* principle B. It is (?) more important to avoid hurting other people's feelings than to tell the truth. It is more important to tell the truth than to avoid punishment. 'More important than' is equivalent to 'better than' in this context in English, so I will call statements of the form: principle A is more important than principle B, 'second-order comparisons'.

Harford Thomas, writing in the *Guardian* (30.IX.1969) of George Orwell's instruction in the skill of writing about politics, said:

His maxims boil down to six:
1. Never use a metaphor, simile or other figure of speech which you are used to seeing in print.
2. Never use a long word where a short one will do.

3. If it is possible to cut out a word, always cut it out.
4. Never use a passive where you can use the active.
5. Never use a foreign phrase, a scientific word, or a jargon word if you can think of any everyday English equivalent.
6. Break any of these rules sooner than say anything outright barbarous.

No. 6 is a paradigm of what I have called a second-order comparison. Not to say anything outright barbarous is (in Orwell's judgment) *more important than* never to use a long word where a short one will do, etc.

Similarly, Polonius's celebrated advice to Laertes (*Hamlet*, I.3.55):

> There, my blessing with thee!
> And these few precepts in thy memory
> Look thou character . . .
>   Beware
> Of entrance to a quarrel, but, being in,
> Bear 't that th' opposed may beware of thee.
> Give every man thine ear, but few thy voice;
> Take each man's censure, but reserve thy judgment.
> Costly thy habit as thy purse can buy,
> But not express'd in fancy; rich, not gaudy;
> For the apparel oft proclaims the man,
> And they in France of the best rank and station
> Are most select and generous, chief in that.
> Neither a borrower, nor a lender be;
> For loan oft loses both itself and friend,
> And borrowing dulls the edge of husbandry.
> This above all: to thine own self be true,
> And it must follow, as the night the day.
> Thou canst not then be false to any man.

'To thine own self be true' would seem here to be used as a second-order comparison. One presumes that Polonius would think it more important for Laertes to dress gaudily if he thought that by so doing he was being true to himself, than to dress in a way which was rich' not gaudy. (Perhaps not, but that is what Polonius *says*.)

Purposive behaviour entails a temporal sequence of events. A person has certain plans and intentions and to achieve these he will be envisaging the possibilities of action and of finding '*means*' towards '*ends*'—which 'ends' may, in their turn, be 'means' towards further 'ends'. Isn't the *real* point of the pattern of purposive behaviour to which the Mechanic's principle is relevant to get from point A to point B in the shortest possible time? Is this not more important than avoiding damage to the batteries of the car? One might argue that whether or not the batteries are damaged is not very important when compared with the fact that to crank the car by hand will lose five precious minutes. However, supposing the agent does not *own* the car, and it has been lent to him by John Doe who has made him promise to start the engine by hand in cold weather? Is it not more important to honour one's promises than to get from point A to point B in the shortest possible time?

Sometimes these problems resolve themselves relatively easily: 'All skills', wrote Aristotle, [11] 'of that kind come under a single "faculty"—a skill in making bridles or any other part of a horse's gear comes under the faculty or art of horsemanship, while horsemanship and every other part of military practice comes under the art of war, and in like manner other arts and techniques are subordinate to yet others—in all these the ends of the master arts are to be preferred to those of the subordinate skills, for it is the former that provide the motive for pursuing the latter.' In these cases one may sketch a hierarchy of different patterns of purposive behaviour, some of which are in the following relationship to one another: the decision about which of two conflicting true principles is more important than the other is taken in accordance with second-order principles in what may (following Aristotle) be called a 'master' pattern of purposive behaviour—but meaning by master in this context no more than that pattern of purposive behaviour by whose principles conflicts between principles in the first may be resolved.

I am not trying to argue that conflicts between true principles can always be resolved by this procedure, only that they sometimes can be.

SUMMARY: Second-order comparisons—of the form: principle A is more important than principle B—may sometimes be used to resolve conflicts between true principles.

3. Is there a Master Art of All?

There is a temptation here to say that this is the point where one can draw the distinction between moral and other principles: that moral principles are *strong* second-order comparisons. A strong comparison, it will be recalled, is one in which the spokesman avers that a certain action C is *the best* way of performing a certain pattern of purposive behaviour. So to say of it that it is a 'moral principle' amounts to saying of a principle that it is either the most important principle there can be, or that it is a member of a class of principles all of which are equally important and more important than any other principles. Although this may well be true, it tells us very little. But there is a variant of this which tells us something, but what it tells us is false. This argument is that the master art of all is the pattern of purposive behaviour we all pursue as *men,* and not as etymologists, dieticians, mechanics, etc., and moral principles are the principles connected with the pattern of purposive behaviour we pursue as men.

It is argued [12] that it is *impossible* that a man's family relationships, his knowledge and mental skills, his sense of justice, his tendency to tell the truth, and his good faith in keeping contracts, should be entirely irrelevant to his 'moral' goodness or badness. Part of what we mean by the word 'moral', when we use the phrase 'moral principles', are just these things. That to define a moral principle in such a way that principles like one ought not to say what is false, and that one ought not to take human life, are not *necessarily* moral principles, is to go beyond the limits of what the English language will allow.

This argument is false for the following reasons. What we decide to be the most important principle, or a member of the class of most important principles, is a matter of choice which cannot be decided *on principle*. In 1940 both Britons and Germans subordinated the business of behaving as men, to the more important business of trying to win the war. We followed Aristotle's dictum: 'The good of the individual is worthwhile. But what is good for a city has a higher, a diviner quality.'[13] Accordingly, men abandoned their homes, sent their wives to work and their children abroad, forsook their professions and allowed their civilian skills to go to seed, imprisoned individuals without trial, shot those who worked for the enemy, released themselves unilaterally from their contracts, set out to kill other human beings and were still judged (and rightly judged) to be good men. Their goodness or badness as men was judged exclusively by reference to their contribution to the war effort. The only good German, said the British, is a dead German. The only good Briton, said the Germans, is a dead Briton. Hitler was a good man according to his lights although we know many of his principles (one of which was that one ought to eliminate the Jews) to have been pernicious.

Moreover, I do not think that such a view about the subordinate importance of man's behaviour as man is confined to populations at war with one another. As I understand the position of a convinced militant Communist in a non-Communist society, it is that all what are conventionally called 'moral principles' (like speaking the truth, caring for one's parents, etc.) are to be considered subordinate to the principles involved in the pattern of purposive behaviour aimed at producing the Revolution. To achieve the Revolution is the most important aim that anyone can have in life.

It is a matter of choice. We can choose to make the behaviour of men as men the master art of all, and judge their performances as etymologists or mechanics or aestheticians as *less important* than their behaviour as men. Or we can choose to make their behaviour as cogs in the machine of state, or in the furtherance of the Revolution, the master art of all, and judge their performance as men in accordance with their utility in that pattern of purposive behaviour.

There is, *in theory,* no reason why we should not judge a

person's performance as a mechanic to be more important than any other pattern of purposive behaviour that he performs. Such a second-order comparison would very much change the pattern of our lives; we would, for instance, have to transform our children's education. Some people, whom we now judge to be good men, we would feel we ought to denounce as deplorable failures. The saints of the past would be the mechanical engineers of genius, and Leo Tolstoy would not be noticed except to be commented upon as a deluded eccentric. We make this sort of second-order comparison now for racehorses, and judge their goodness or badness solely upon the basis of how fast they gallop over selected distances at a handful of race-courses in the world. To win these races is more important than any qualities of beauty, good manners or adaptability they may possess. It should be noted that some governments the world over still make the same sort of judgments about selected classes of their own citizens.

How does it come about, then, that part of what we seem to mean by a 'good man' is just this: that he tells the truth, loves his children, honours his parents, etc.? My answer is that it is *contingently* the case we are more often in a 1970 situation than a 1940 situation: that philosophers whom we admire choose to denigrate the situation in which a man finds himself used as a pawn in a machine; and that when philosophers find themselves in a 1940 situation they have no time to philosophise. In the end it comes down to how we choose to order the importance of patterns of purposive behaviour—and this cannot be done on principle.

It is therefore a delusion to hope that one will be able to find a way to describe the difference between moral principles and others by positing a master art of all (which is more general than any other) whose principles are the most important of all, because to do so itself involves making a choice: choosing which the master art is to be. We may all think that we know what the right choice is, but this does not solve the problem on principle.

SUMMARY: A decision as to what (if any) is the master art of all does not solve the question of which are moral principles and which not.

4. *Conflicts between Experts*

One of the troubles with second-order principles is that the results at which they may be alleged to be directed tend to be so nebulous (either by design or omission) that they have no possibility of being other than inane. To what end ought one not to say anything outright barbarous in writing about politics? To what end ought one to be true to oneself above all other principles? To what end is what is good for a nation or a city more important than what is good for the individual? To what results are these second-order principles directed?

Since the result tends to be nebulous, teleological reasons are not convincing. Received reasons tend to be the only reasons which can convincingly be given: that George Orwell or Shakespeare (in the guise of one of his characters) or Aristotle taught these principles and that they are universally acknowledged to be experts in their particular patterns of purposive behaviour (whatever these may have been).

But what if these experts advocate conflicting second-order principles—how does one then choose between them? The common jibe 'What does *he* know about it' has great persuasive force. If I were to answer the descriptive question (rather than the normative question of how one ought to choose between experts) I would guess that impulses like *loyalty* to a teacher play a large part in the process. And we tend (perhaps wrongly) to be guided by the opinions of other experts in the same field of purposive behaviour about their contemporaries' expertise.

Our assessment of an agent's judgment of his own work is illuminating in this context. Why is it that there is a peculiar significance in the fact that G. E. Moore judged his book on *Ethics* to be a better book than *Principia Ethica*? Why is it especially important that Evelyn Waugh judged that he was a better novelist in his forties than in his sixties? Why is it so important that, before he hanged himself, Judas Iscariot judged that he was a bad man?

There is often this very great vagueness in being able to define the result of a pattern of purposive behaviour: i.e. over precisely *what* it is that the pattern of purposive behaviour is trying to achieve. What gives the agent a special authority in comparing his own acts with his other actions is that he knows what he is trying to achieve in a way which no one else can. It is for this same reason that we tend to value very highly the opinion of other experts in the same field about their competitors' work. They, we feel, ought to know what it is that the particular pattern of purposive behaviour is getting at.

On the normative question of how one ought to choose between experts when they advocate conflicting second-order principles, there is no *logical* reason why we should not be able to compare them one with another. One could advance the principle that one ought always to follow the advice of the expert who was richest in financial terms; or the expert who weighed the least; or the expert with the fewest hairs on his chest; or the expert who could throw the discus furthest. But there is no obvious reason *why* one should choose any of these criteria as the hallmark of wisdom.

This is so even in the case of their own particular skill. It might be thought sensible to choose the advice of the expert who could throw the discus the furthest in the skill of discus-throwing; or the advice of the expert with the most money in the skill of money-making. But many excellent performers are poor teachers —and insofar that the argument runs that the excellent performers must advocate the right principles because they are excellent performers, the argument becomes circular.

SUMMARY: When experts conflict in the second-order principles they advocate, one ought not to choose between them on principle.

CHAPTER SIX

Moral Principles

1. *The Importance of Motive*

ONE of the earlier contentious features of my argument may
now be put in this way. People find themselves in a relation
of apprenticeship to someone else in all patterns of purposive
behaviour from solemn ones, as when they cannot make up their
minds about what they ought to do in life, to trivial ones like
assuaging their hunger at breakfast. At one extreme the priesthood
devotes a large part of its activities to giving people instruction on
how they ought to conduct their whole lives. At the other,
people can (and do) give and receive instruction on entirely
trivial matters like how to blow their noses. The function of
principles in situations of apprenticeship is always the same: to
assist people in achieving the best possible performance of the
pattern of purposive behaviour in question.

I am therefore arguing that a trivial principle like the Aesthetician's one ought not to wear a pink tie with a magenta shirt has
the same sort of function as a solemn moral principle. Both are
used in this teaching-learning process in connection with patterns
of purposive behaviour, although (of course) these patterns are
directed towards achieving very different results. Both have the
same logic. What makes some of them moral principles and not
others?

Let us again treat the principle that one ought not to say what
is false, as a paradigm of a moral principle—in a way that the
Aesthetician's principle clearly is not. Now, although the no-
falsehoods principle usually expresses a moral principle, there are
contexts in which it seems not to do so. Further, there are
contexts in which the Aesthetician's principle could occur as a
moral principle. In some contexts—special cases, perhaps, but
significant—the no-falsehoods principle and the Aesthetician's

principle can creep out of the class in which each of them is usually catalogued and slip into the other's pigeon-hole.

Preparatory to sending him into the witness box, his lawyer may say to an unfastidious client, 'Under oath one ought not to say what is false because to do so is perjury, which will get you a prison sentence if you are found out.' Or a colleague may mutter a variant of the Businessman's principle to his partner before an important conference, 'If the bankers get an inkling that they are being deceived, they will not grant a loan, so one ought not to say what is false.' I would argue that in these contexts a moral principle is not at stake, but something else—the law of England in one case, and a variant of the Businessman's principle in the other.

The counterpart example is, of necessity, somewhat contrived. But suppose that wearing a pink tie with a magenta shirt were a kind of 'skin-head's' uniform and became the hall-mark of a club of young drug-takers. I might then say to my children, 'One ought not to wear a pink tie with a magenta shirt', with all the force of a moral principle. 'One ought not to wear a black shirt' when uttered in many contexts in England in the 1930's, and 'One ought to wear a black sash' when uttered in some contexts in South Africa recently, have both in their ways attained the status of moral principles. In some contexts, principles which appear to refer to dress have (in fact) to do with morals. How does this come about?

If I am right that it is possible for the no-falsehoods principle, in some contexts, to express something other than a moral principle; and it is possible for the Aesthetician's principle, in some contexts, to express a moral principle; then there is an important consequence. It follows that, in trying to find the difference between moral principles and others, it will be useless to examine the form taken by different principles or the uses to which they are put in the language in the hope that these may provide a clue. Both have the same form and the same logic. Whether a principle is a moral principle or not will depend upon *the particular context* in which it occurs. What we have to do is to find the difference between the situations in which someone uses the no-falsehoods principle in the moral sense, and the situations in which someone uses it in the non-moral sense. The same *mutatis mutandis* with the Aesthetician's principle.

To specify the result at which a principle is aimed (i.e. to give one's motive for a performance of a pattern of purposive behaviour) is not the same thing as to give teleological reasons for adhering to a principle. Both involve peeping into the future, but the latter activity involves giving a general explanation of the results likely to follow from adopting a principle whenever it occurs relevantly in a situation of apprenticeship, whereas to supply a motive simply gives the specific reason why the agent is engaged in a pattern of purposive behaviour at that particular time.

It is a feature of supplying a motive for performing a pattern of purposive behaviour that it may lay itself open to questioning in the following manner (often becoming more and more eroded by inanity on the way):

Agent: I want to look fashionable. One ought not to wear a magenta shirt with a pink tie if one wants to look fashionable, so I must not do so.

Questioner: Why do you want to look fashionable?

Agent: Because I want to be attractive to members of the opposite sex and one ought to look fashionable if one wants to be attractive to members of the opposite sex.

Questioner: Why do you want to be attractive to members of the opposite sex?

Agent: Because I want to get asked to parties, and one ought to be attractive to members of the opposite sex if one wants to get asked to parties.

Questioner: Why do you want to get asked to parties?

Agent: Because I want to meet more people and enlarge my experience of life, and one ought to go to parties if one wants to meet people.

Questioner :	Why do you want to enlarge your experience of life?
Agent :	Because I want to be happy, and enlarging one's experience of life makes one happier.
Questioner :	But why do you want to be happy?
Agent :	Because one just *ought* to want to be happy.

The above account is laboured and unreal. We normally have to spell out each step in the argument in the way outlined only when we are explaining things to idiots and very young children. Why ought one to have worn a black sash? Because it was the hall-mark of those who resisted Apartheid and one just ought to resist Apartheid. In the same way one ought not to say what is false, not *because* to do so may jeopardise the chances of getting an overdraft, or land one in jail for perjury—but because one just ought not to say what is false. The action is to be judged on its own, irrespective of its consequences.

It is my argument that it is the *absence* of a motive in adopting a principle, or 'sticking at' a principle in a particular context, that is the test of whether an agent is using a principle as a moral principle or not. When someone is using a principle with some result in view, he is not using it as a moral principle. When a person is no longer prepared to give a reason for adopting a principle, then he is using it as a moral principle in that context.

By saying that a person (the agent) is no longer prepared to give reasons, I am not arguing that he *cannot* justify the principle with teleological and/or received reasons. Of course he can do this, but these reasons are not **his** only reasons for adopting the principle in that situation. The agent has no motive. This is the fourth and last thing I have to say which is (I think) different from what most philosophers would argue.

Why is it, then, that so many people look upon the no-false-hoods principle as a moral principle no matter in what context it occurs; and that so few (if any) look upon the Aesthetician's principle as a moral principle? I would argue that it is because in England in 1970 so many more wise people would take their stand upon the no-falsehoods principle than would 'stick at' the Aesthetician's principle. It is illuminating in this context to consider the changes that have occurred in the recent past in these wise people's attitude to sexual activity outside marriage. Half a century ago, the received view was that it was *morally* wrong to copulate outside the marriage partnership; now (I would guess) the received view is that it is not morally wrong, although it may produce undesirable consequences.

There is an argument that some men have *no* principles—in the sense that such a man holds no principles in the way that I have suggested that someone must hold them for them to qualify as moral principles. (I would suspect that at least some of the people who argue this way hold at least one principle as a moral principle: namely that one ought not to hold moral principles, but this is by the way.) This is a perfectly consistent view. Just as certainly, there are many people who wish to have standards of conduct laid down for them by their betters. These people, I would argue, hold at least one moral principle, namely that one ought always to follow the principles of conduct laid down by the Church, or by wise men.

So many wise men in our schools of thought believe the no-falsehoods principle to be, *for them,* a true moral principle, that we have come to look upon it as a moral principle irrespective of the context in which it occurs. The day may yet dawn when wise men will look upon the Aesthetician's principle in just the same way. At that time the Aesthetician's principle would have attained the status of a moral principle. Some people indeed hold aesthetic principles as *moral* principles. Wittgenstein we are told knew that one ought to like Schubert's music, and became very cross if this were questioned.

SUMMARY: The distinction between moral principles and others lies in the context in which these respectively occur. One ought to treat a principle as a moral principle in the context where the agent adopts it with no motive.

2. *The Decision to 'back' a Principle against All Comers*

Let us re-examine this argument from another angle by looking again at contexts in which principles are clearly *not* being used as moral principles. Any principle which is being used as a means to an end is not being used as a moral principle in the sense in which I have described moral principles. Thus, when a colleague says to his partner in the bank parlour: 'Look here! One ought not to say what is false, because if a banker gets an inkling that he is being deceived, one does not get the loan.' His partner may reply: 'But old Richard Roe has told me (and he ought to know because he is on their Board, after all) that they do not expect one to tell the truth about one's private life.' It is possible that in this situation, the colleague may say: 'Oh, well! if Richard Roe really told you *that*, say what you like about your private life,' or, 'if it really will not hinder our getting the loan, say what you like about that.' Similarly with the Aesthetician's principle on those occasions when it occurs, for example, when someone is getting dressed. It is possible that his wife may suggest to him that he should cut a dash by wearing a pink tie with his magenta shirt. 'But,' he may argue, 'one ought not to wear a pink tie with a magenta shirt, they would laugh me to scorn in the Common Room if I did.' Or: 'But the *Tailor and Cutter* would flay me alive if they saw me wearing a pink tie with a magenta shirt.'

Such possible instances are clearly distinguishable from others. In the bank parlour a colleague may say to his partner: 'One ought not to say what is false. If a banker gets an inkling that one is deceiving him, one will not get the loan.' His partner may reply as follows: 'But old Richard Roe (and he ought to know, he is on their Board) has told me that they do not expect one to tell the truth about one's private life.' Then the conversation may take a different turn to the previous instance. 'I do not care a fig for old Richard Roe's opinions,' his colleague may reply, 'the fact is that one ought not to say what is false.' 'But,' his partner may answer, 'if I tell them all about X, we will not get the loan and we'll all be ruined.' 'That is as may be,' the stern answer may come back, 'the fact is that one ought not to say what is false. One's duty at all times and in all places is to tell the whole truth. That is all there is to it, and that is my last word on the subject.' (One may note in passing that it is in situations like this that men resign as a matter of *principle*.)

It is, I suppose, just conceivable (but unlikely in this day and age) that one could hear the following analogous conversation between husband and wife about the Aesthetician's principle. 'But, darling, nowadays the fashion is to shock people not to please them aesthetically. So your dress must be unconventional in order to shock.' Answer: 'Fashion be damned! If I have to wear a magenta shirt, I will *not* wear a pink tie with it, because one ought not to wear a pink tie with a magenta shirt.' Wife: 'But, darling, the *Tailor and Cutter* says that the best dressed men nowadays often wear pink ties with a magenta shirt'. Answer: 'I so not care a fig for the *Tailor and Cutter's* opinion. This is a far deeper matter of principle than that. Old standards are being undermined. It is Bolshevism in disguise, etc., etc.'

The crucial point is that in some contexts the reasons (both teleological and received) which ought to be given to establish the truth-value of a principle have ceased to be of any importance to the agent who advances a principle. In these contexts, he believes in the principle *as an end in itself*. A moral principle is, by definition, an *incomplete* principle in the sense I described in IV.v. Such principles are being used as articles of faith, and one might describe the use of principles in this way as clinging to them as an *act of faith*, if this phrase did not contain undesirable and irrelevant religious overtones. I shall describe such a decision as a decision to 'back' a principle against all comers. Although reason may enter into such a decision, as in backing a racehorse, the final step is essentially an irrational commitment.

I am not arguing that received and teleological reasons may not, in the end, cause someone to cease to back certain principles as moral principles (which he has previously backed against all comers). People's moral views change not only in an individual's own lifetime, but in the same school of thought over the years.

All I am arguing is that it is necessary to the situation in which a principle is being used by an agent as a *moral* principle that, in that context, at that time, he should be backing the principle against all comers. Further, I think one ought to describe those principles and those principles only which a person habitually backs against all comers as his moral principles, notwithstanding that he may sometimes use them in situations of choice in which they may occur as non-moral principles. For anyone, his moral principles are the principles whose truth-value he knows, irrespective of teleological and received reasons.

SUMMARY: One ought to describe those principles and those principles only which a person usually backs against all comers as his moral principles. They are, by definition, incomplete principles. For anyone, his moral principles are the principles whose truth-values he knows, irrespective of teleological and received reasons.

3. *Our Ignorance of our own Motives*

There is at least one powerful argument against this account of the borderline between moral principles and non-moral principles to which I think I have a satisfactory answer. There are, no doubt, other powerful arguments against it which I have not thought of.

There are many principles with which some of us unhesitatingly indoctrinate our children which would seem to fall within the class of moral principles by my definition. That is to say that we would back them against all comers, but they seem to be aimed at no result; and we do not pursue them because of respect for any teacher who has advanced them. They are often connected with manners and etiquette: e.g. that a man ought to give up his seat in the bus for a lady; that one ought not to call a lavatory 'the toilet'; or that one ought not to shoot on Sundays, and if one must shoot, then one ought only to shoot vermin. Now, however one looks at them, these are not *moral* principles. So it follows that my account of the borderline between moral principles and others is wrong.

My answer to this is that the true position in the contexts in which these principles come to be used is obscured by our frightening ignorance of our own motives. As I mentioned at the very beginning of this book we all perform patterns of purposive behaviour whose goals we do not recognise unless and until our attention is called to them: *speaking* is an example of this. 'Civilisation advances', said Whitehead [14] 'by extending the number of important operations we can perform without thinking about them.' What is more alarming to our own knowledge of ourselves is that we are continually being offered new (and sometimes satisfying) explanations of what our goals and ambitions *really* are when we had previously thought them different. Freud has, I think, successfully convinced many of us of the unfulfilled sexual goals and ambitions behind some of our oddest conduct. But, post-Freud, the popularity of books like Ardrey's *The Territorial Imperative* and Morris's *The Human Ape* and *The Human Zoo* shows that there is more ground in this field still to be explored.

Without going the whole way with every hypothesis put forward by anthropologists (professional or amateur) I am convinced that many of us hold as a moral principle that one ought to conform to the (harmless) mores of one's group. The evidence for this distasteful proposition is skilfully marshalled by William H. Whyte in his book *The Organization Man*. He concludes that: 'The organization man's emphasis on the group, I have been maintaining, is not a temporary phenomenon dictated by external necessity: it is a response to what he feels is a moral imperative, and more and more he is openly articulating it.' [15]

It is as a means towards the end defined by this moral principle that we find ourselves teaching our male children to stand up in buses; not to call a lavatory, the 'toilet'; and to shoot only vermin on Sundays. No doubt this admission accurately plots my place in society on the basis of age, class and *prejudices* (which is, of course, a pejorative way of describing 'misconceived principles'). No doubt the moral principle is itself misconceived: but I share it with a number of other people. When in Rome, say others, do as the Romans do—and my moral principle is not very different from this adage.

So if I am asked by my child why one ought to stand up during the playing of one's National Anthem in a public place, or why men ought to get up in buses to give their place to women, etc., I would answer that these principles are not inane, as I suggested earlier, but are true because they are directed to the result of conforming to the (harmless) mores of one's group. I can think of teleological and received reasons in support of this principle— but even if someone shows me that I am wrong about some of these, I think I would still hold that one ought to conform to the (harmless) mores of one's group. The truth is that I am a Conformist: I can be truthfully described as such because I hold this particular moral principle to be true.

SUMMARY: We are frighteningly ignorant of our own motives, and this is why we sometimes mistake for a moral principle (by my definition) something which is really not a moral principle but a means towards an end we had overlooked or deceived ourselves about.

4. *Is Moral Philosophy founded on a Mistake?*

In 1912 Prichard wrote his justly celebrated article in *Mind* called 'Does Moral Philosophy Rest on a Mistake?' He came to the conclusion that moral philosophy rested on a mistake because, although in moral philosophy we are always looking for a reason for behaving in the way we know we ought to behave, the truth is that 'The sense of obligation to do, or of the rightness of, an action of a particular kind is absolutely underivative or immediate . . . We do not come to appreciate an obligation by argument, i.e. by a process of non-moral thinking, our sense of the rightness of an act is not a conclusion from our appreciation of the goodness of it or of anything else . . . When or rather so far as, we act from a sense of obligation, we have no purpose or end.' [16]

I argue that Prichard was right, although not in the comprehensive way in which I suspect that he thought he was right. I argue only that what distinguishes a moral principle (in most of the contexts in which it occurs) like one ought not to say what is false, from a non-moral principle (in most of the contexts in which this principle occurs) like one ought not to wear a pink tie with a magenta shirt is that, usually, someone advancing the latter would be prepared to reject the principle if it could be shown to his satisfaction that it did not conduce to the desired result, and was not supported by the spokesman he admired; but that anyone who uses the no-falsehoods principle may very well adopt it irrespective of the result and the opinion of others, *as an end in itself*. In the situation in which this occurs, it is being used as a moral principle and is backed irrespective of teleological reasons and irrespective of the exhortations of wise men opposed to it.

If my account of moral principles is correct it is always a matter of the agent's own convictions whether or not a principle is a moral principle in the context in which it occurs. For many people (e.g. a certain type of convinced Theist) the *only* moral principle will be that one ought to do God's Will. For them, that one ought not to say what is false, will be a *means* towards the *end* of achieving God's Will (because the Eighth Commandment forbids all false testimony, rash judgments and lies).

Moore, at the time he wrote *Principia Ethica,* held two moral principles (in my sense) which exercised a profound influence on his contemporaries:

> By far the most valuable things, which we know or can imagine, are certain states of consciousness which may be roughly described as the pleasures of human intercourse and the enjoyment of beautiful objects. No one probably, who has asked himself the question has ever doubted that personal affection and the appreciation of what is beautiful in Art or Nature, are good in themselves; nor if we consider strictly what things are worth having purely for their own sakes, does it appear probable that anyone will think anything else has nearly so great a value as the things which are included under these two heads. [17]

But people's moral principles are not always as innocuous as Moore's. Some very wicked moral principles have been held in our own time: e.g. that one ought to eliminate the Jews, and that one ought to silence those of a different political persuasion to oneself (which is a variant of the old theme that one ought to persecute heretics). It is not very illuminating in what purports to be a work of philosophy to catalogue the various sorts of moral principles which have been held. But it is worth pointing out again that, by my account, there is no logical inconsistency in the position of the individual who holds no moral principles. He simply affirms that there is no principle which he knows to be true irrespective of teleological and received reasons.

From my description of a moral principle one very important conclusion emerges. If someone is convinced of a moral principle it is useless to 'reason' with him—for by definition he holds the view he holds irrespective of the teleological and received reasons for it. We have, in the current controversy over the abolition of hanging, an example of the uselessness of argument in this context. There are those who are more revolted by the thought of the punishment than they are by the fact of the crime; and those who are more revolted by the fact of the crime than they are by the thought of the punishment. Irrespective of what the 'statistics' reveal, or of those spokesmen who argue either way, there are those of us who are more revolted by the thought of hanging even a guilty murderer than we are revolted (however *saddened* we may be) by the fact that he has committed murder. But there are other equally sincere people who believe differently. When it comes to legislation, if we believe in democracy, we must stand up and be counted, for it is useless to argue any more. When it comes to morals, it is still useless to argue, for each man is entitled to his own view: but, to some of us, these are the most important things in life and are not decided on a show of hands.

In describing myself as a Conformist in the previous section, I was doing no more than making explicit the obvious fact that it is (among other things which they cannot help, like the colour of their hair) by their moral principles that individuals are distinguishable from one another. To describe someone as a Roman Catholic means that he holds as a moral principle that one ought to subscribe on matters of faith and 'morals' to what the Church ordains. ('Morals' in this context meaning one's behaviour as a man and not as an etymologist, dietician or probation officer.) To describe someone as a Logical Positivist means that he holds the principle (roughly) that one ought to predicate truth or falsehood only of mathematical propositions and scientific hypotheses. To describe someone as a utilitarian means (among other things) that he believes that one ought to maximise happiness as a moral principle; as a radical, that he believes as a **moral** principle that one ought to promote change; and so on.

Some of the most serious moral decisions an individual faces in his life may be connected with these descriptions. When someone makes up his mind to throw off the beliefs of his parents —thus breaking the principle that one ought to conform to the (harmless) mores of one's group—and turn Roman Catholic (if he has been brought up in some other religion); or turn radical (if he has been brought up conservative), he has to make a decision that the principle one ought to subscribe on matters of faith and morals to what the Church ordains (or that one ought to promote change) is *more important than* the principle that one ought to conform to the mores of one's group. These, together with decisions about what we shall do in life—whether we shall become etymologists, doctors, probation officers, or postmen—and whom we shall marry—are (when we are lucky enough to have a choice) the biggest decisions we ever make.

Precisely what moral principles any description entails will often be a matter of some delicacy. There are as many possible permutations and combinations of moral principles which an individual may consistently hold as there are people in any population, and this is what makes for the fascinating variety in men. One of the things this book is *not* trying to attempt is to make it easier for people to take moral decisions. I argue that such a programme would be misconceived. For it is because there is such an infinite variety of possible combinations, that people are as interesting as they are.

If someone were to succeed in solving the problem of how moral decisions ought to be taken, and could transmit this vision to the world, everyone would (presumably) sooner or later come to hold the same moral principles and so become more and more alike. This would (to me) be a matter, not for congratulation, but for great regret.

SUMMARY : Prichard was right in saying that when we act in accordance with a moral principle 'we have no purpose or end.' Man's infinite variety stems from the fact that his moral principles may be unique to himself.

5. *Are Moral Principles completely Arbitrary?*

My central thesis is that the distinctive mark of moral principles is that they are not justified in terms of their conduciveness to some desired end. Does this mean, a critic may justifiably inquire, that moral judgments are completely arbitrary as a result of being unreasoned? Because if this is the argument it is clearly absurd.

'Arbitrary' (according to the *O.E.D.*) means 'based on mere opinion or preference, hence, capricious'. I am not arguing that moral principles are capricious. A moral principle is just as much a principle as any other. All principles can be supported by teleological and received reasoning. So, in the sense in which I understand the words 'arbitrary', 'capricious' and 'unreasoned' these apply as little to moral principles as they do to other principles.

But that any person should choose to select some principles and not others as *his* moral principles is, to my way of thinking, 'arbitrary', 'capricious' or 'unreasoned'—as long as these words are not understood in a derogatory sense. In any school of thought individuals will adhere to moral principles (or to no moral principles) in a pattern which will approximate closer to a random scatter than to a coherent system.

Anyone who plays cricket will be familiar with the concept of behaviour which is 'not cricket'—not in the sense that the behaviour is against the rules, or that it will not conduce to winning the match, but in the sense that one just ought not to do it. For example, a bowler ought not to run out the batsman at his end by feigning a delivery of the ball and then whipping off the bails. Moreover to some professional cricketers (i.e. those to whom cricket is more important than any other activity in their lives) a principle such as this may well, to them, be a moral principle.

Parallel examples may be found in nearly every profession. One ought not to deal before one's client if one is a stockbroker; one ought not to pinch another firm's successful authors, if one is a publisher; one ought not to devote more time to television appearances than to academic work, if one is a university lecturer; and so on.

In case I am thought to be exaggerating on this point, I quote from two letters to *The Times* on August 13, 1971, following the effective devaluation of the dollar:

GOLD AND GUILT

From Mr. Paul Bareau.
Sir, Under the heading 'Gold and Guilt Complexes' (August 13), your Economics Editor, Mr. Peter Jay, quotes with approval the dictum of his mentor, Professor Kaldor, 'devalue early and devalue often'. As for the guilt, he heaps it on those who believe in and have tried to strive for the stability of money.

Here is a strangely perverted allocation of praise and criticism. These are the morals of Oz translated to the world of economics.

Does it occur to Mr. Jay that inflation is *evil in itself,* a corrupting influence responsible for much of the economic disarray and personal distress around us? The guilt should be worn by those who have acquiesced in and contribute to the persistent erosion in the value of money—be they politicians, central bankers, trade union bosses, university professors or economics editors.

Yours faithfully,
PAUL BAREAU,
Reform Club, Pall Mall, SW1.
August 13.

From Canon H. H. M. Hallidie Smith.
Sir, In 1919, at the height of the mark devaluation, I was billeted on a German colonel in Cologne. When his pay cheque came on the first of each month he never knew whether it would buy rations for a month, a week or a day. All he did know was that without the payment in British money that he received he could not survive.

Perhaps when disciples of the Kaldor doctrine retire on half pay they too may argue that *there is an immoral dishonesty in devaluation.*
I have the honour to be, Sir, your obedient servant,

H. H. M. HALLIDIE SMITH,
12, Wingate Way, Trumpington,
Cambridge.
August 15.
(My italics.)

The moral is clear: to some economists, professional and amateur, it is *immoral* to acquiesce in or contribute to a devaluation of the currency *irrespective* of the consequences.

Every profession has rules which conduce to no particular end, but by which other professionals will sort the sheep from the goats. They are of critical importance in the profession, but are often a source of mystification (and/or amusement) to the non-professional. What is so very wrong if a bowler takes advantage of the rules, and runs out the batsman at his end? He *is* playing the game—but the gravamen of the charge against him is that he just ought not to have done it. What is so wrong about the erosion of any currency provided it resolves inconsistencies in the international monetary system?

Per contra, what seems to us (in the West) to be pre-eminently a matter of *morals,* may well seem to other civilisations a much more trivial matter. From the accounts of the way the Japanese behaved to their prisoners of war during the 1939–1945 War, it is clear that they took an entirely different view about the sanctity of human life from most Europeans. To shoot unarmed prisoners of war was, to them, the right way to behave. It was a kindness to their victims to release them from the humiliation and degradation of capture.

To some philosophers, what would strike a non-philosopher as an entirely trivial matter can become a moral matter. Norman Malcolm recounts how one day he and Wittgenstein quarrelled. Wittgenstein later wrote about the occasion to Malcolm:[18] '. . . Whenever I thought of you I couldn't help thinking of a particular incident which seemed to me very important. You and I were walking along the river towards the railway bridge and we had a heated discussion in which you made a remark about "national character" that shocked me by its primitiveness . . .' i.e. it was *immoral.* Quite so, the philosopher in us may say. But *only* philosophers would understand why Wittgenstein would want to make a moral issue of it. It is precisely because our moral principles are not justifiable in terms of their conduciveness to some desired result that we get so emotionally involved in them. Were we able to justify them rationally, there would be no need to get emotionally involved.

SUMMARY: All principles can be supported by reasons, but in any school of thought, individuals will adhere to moral principles (or to no moral principles) in a pattern which will approximate closer to a random scatter than to a coherent system.

CHAPTER SEVEN

Rival Theories

1. *The Prescriptive Theory of Ethics*

ONE of the philosophical comparisons to which I subscribe is that, in philosophy, it is more important to say something intelligible but false, than to say something which is true but so careful that it (in effect) says nothing. For example, as in another context one can say: 'Either there are four people in this room or there are not four people in this room,' so in philosophy one can say: 'Either this is such and such or, alternatively, it is not such and such.' Philosophical language can be made very difficult to understand, and it requires no great ingenuity to express the alternative in a way so devious that the reader is left with the impression that something profound is there, when nothing has been said at all. Following John Wisdom, I subscribe to the maxim: No stakes, no winnings.

I am most anxious not to have said nothing in this book. What I set out to do was to give a *sufficient* answer (not necessarily the only possible answer) to the conundrum of what it is that distinguishes moral from other principles. It is falsification that has the logical force attributed by the Logical Positivists to verification. [19] Once the views of a philosopher are so safe that nothing can falsify them, they cease to be of any use in getting clearer on things. As comparisons they are inane. My views would be false if the prescriptivist theory of ethics was true; so I shall begin by trying to show that the prescriptivist theory is false.

Take the following statements:

Only tiny babies mess their pants.

This stuff is called 'spaghetti', not 'bascotti'.

Some people breakfast off a Prairie Oyster when they have a hang-over.

Stirling Moss always cranks his car in cold weather.

John Doe passed his Bar Finals in six weeks by taking a course at Gibson & Weldon.

The trend-setters predicate truth and falsehood only of tautologies and scientific hypotheses.

Drug-taking is habit-forming; whisky-drinking less so.

Only someone who likes cinema organs would dare play the 'forty-eight' to a German audience on anything other than a harpsichord.

The Eighth Commandment forbids telling anyone a lie.

It is just not done to wear a pink tie with a magenta shirt.

Most of these I take not to be prescriptive statements, but factual descriptions. Any of them could appear in some contexts in which no one was prescribing anything to anyone. Thus, when his son spots Richard Roe walking away with his legs apart after a long tiring ride on a horse, John Doe may reply to his son's question: 'No, only tiny babies mess their pants.' Someone on the island of Tristan da Cunha (where they make bascotti) may say pointing to a photograph of a plate of spaghetti: 'This stuff is called "spaghetti", not "bascotti".' And so on.

Now, although these are factual descriptions, there are many contexts in which they could occur in which they would be the precise equivalent of the Nanny's (and the other) principles that I have been discussing throughout this book. In these contexts they would prescribe action. In other contexts they would simply give some information and prescribe nothing.

It is my view that comparisons also supply information. The Mark III comparisons make it most explicit. If one wants to stay clean, one uses the pot. If one wants to be understood, one calls that stuff 'spaghetti', etc. As Urmson says: 'On the ordinary occasions of life to tell somebody that something is good is not to attempt to secure agreement in attitude but to supply a useful piece of information.' [20]

The view that I am anxious to show is wrong is most succinctly put forward on p. 1 of Hare's *Language of Morals* where he says: 'The language of morals is one sort of prescriptive language.' I argue that this is false because the language of morals is only prescriptive when it occurs in a special sort of context: in what I have called a situation of apprenticeship. If Desmond Shawe-Taylor says that the Toscanini recording of *Falstaff* is the best available, this (as it stands) is just a piece of information. But if he is one of my mentors in musical appreciation and I am choosing a recording of *Falstaff*, then I can validly infer from this information that I *ought* to pick the Toscanini recording. It is because of the relationship in which I am to Desmond Shawe-Taylor that the information guides my choice, not because the language he talks is prescriptive.

The reason we are deluded into supposing that the language of morals is a variety of prescriptive language is that we are, so much more often than we are prepared to admit, on the one hand uncertain how best to perform a pattern of purposive behaviour; and on the other hand, so certain how something ought to be done that we volunteer information to our school of thought without being asked. In such situations, comparisons have the force of commands.

So my argument against the prescriptivists is this: you say that the language of morals is a variety of prescriptive language and I would not deny that it often occurs in situations where it has the force of a command. But then some descriptive factual statements sometimes occur in situations where they have the force of a command. Are we to say of these statements that they are a variety of prescriptive language? If so, to say of the language of morals that it is a variety of prescriptive language does not tell one very much about the language of morals. If not, how else do these descriptive factual statements differ from the language of morals? And any explanation will lead us back to the beginning of this argument.

SUMMARY: The prescriptivist account of the language of morals is wrong.

2. *The Lawyer's Conception of Moral Rules*

One of the functions of a true principle is that it shall indicate to someone in a situation of apprenticeship what he ought to do when faced with a particular sort of decision.

An argument against this view runs as follows. It may be called the lawyers' conception of moral rules because, on this view, as in the case of *legal* judgments, it is theoretically impossible that principles shall conflict. If they *appear* to conflict it is simply that the House of Lords (or other final Court of Appeal) has had no opportunity of stating what the 'true' law on the point is. Thus Hare, describing why it is that, when we decide for good reason not in a particular instance to adopt the principle one ought not to say what is false, writes:

> we say . . . 'Speak the truth in general, but there are certain classes of cases in which this principle does not hold; for example, you may say what is false in order to save life, and there are other exceptions which you must learn to recognise' . . . For what we are doing in allowing classes of exceptions is to make the principle, not looser, but more rigorous . . . Thus, far from principles like 'Never say what is false' being in some way by nature irredeemably loose, it is part of our moral development to turn them from provisional principles into precise principles with their exceptions definitely laid down; this process is, of course, never completed, but it is always going on in any individual lifetime. [21]

Now, if it is true that this process is never completed, it is true that the principle one ought not to say what is false never indicates what he ought to do to someone faced with a decision to make; because whenever a principle seems to occur non-vacuously in some situation, there is no means of telling whether this is not a new 'exception' to the rule.

It is only lawyers who need a theory in which all situations are unambiguously covered by legal judgments which never, even in theory, conflict. What happens in ordinary life is that principles often conflict with one another. It is not that you may say what is false in order to save life. You may *not* say what is false, but the principle that one ought to save life is *more important*. We allow one principle to over-ride the other. I am not therefore committing the mistake of supposing that the principle one ought not to say what is false is 'loose' in some way. It is as rigorous as may be. But it seems to me to be more sensible to regard some principles as conflicting with one another in some contexts than to talk of an unending class of possible exceptions to a principle. But, if the lawyer's conception of moral rules is right, my argument is false: for all principles will (in my language) be *inane as to action*.

SUMMARY: One should eschew the lawyers' conception of moral rules.

3. *A Scientific Conception of Morals*

Another conception of ethics which, if it is true, falsifies my argument is what I shall call the scientific conception of morals. It is argued by R. B. Braithwaite in *An Empiricist's View of the Nature of Religious Belief*: '. . . an advanced science', he points out, 'has progressed far beyond its natural history stage; it makes use in its explanatory hypotheses of concepts of a high degree of abstractness and at a far remove from experience. These theoretical concepts are given a meaning by the place they occupy in a deductive system consisting of hypotheses of different degrees of generality in which the least general hypotheses, deducible from the more general ones, are generalisations of observable fact.' [22]

This is the model to which moral philosophers are invited to aspire. It should be pointed out that the weakest rule of inference required in this sort of deductive system is the *modus tollendo tollens*: from the denial of the implicate, the denial of the implicans follows. If p, then q. Not q; therefore not p. I say the 'weakest' rule of inference, for, if this did not hold, scientific laws could not be falsified by experience. Every experiment may be said to be planned only in order to give the facts a chance of disproving the hypothesis it has been designed to test. Nothing about the truth or falsehood of the law that all swans are white would follow from the discovery of black swans in Australia, were the *modus tollendo tollens* not valid.

On the scientific conception, an ideal moral system is considered to be like a deductive system used in an advanced science. I quote from Braithwaite once more: 'Not all expressions of intentions will be moral assertions: for the notion of morality to be applicable it is necessary either that the policy of action intended by the asserter should be a general policy (e.g. the policy of utilitarianism) or that it should be subsumable under a general policy which the asserter intends to follow and which he would give as the reason for his specific intention.' In other words that one's principles should be ordered in a nice tidy hierarchy like the laws of physics, starting from the most general principles (like the Greatest Happiness Principle) which are the reasons for more specific ones, which (in their turn) are reasons for the principles we employ when we are coming to day-to-day decisions.

In any deductive system of the kind used in an advanced science, the various hypotheses are (or should be) *consistent* with one another. The first argument against the scientific conception of morals is that it seems impossible to reconcile with the fact that, as we have seen, one of the most obvious facts of life is that principles frequently conflict with one another.

But more than this. Were a scientific deductive system to be comparable with a moral deductive system, then the rules of inference used in scientific reasoning and in moral reasoning ought to have some sort of identity. But, as we have seen, the *modus tollendo tollens* does not ensure a valid inference from general principles to more specific principles. It does *not* follow from the falsehood of the principle that one ought not to kill murderers, that the principle one ought not to kill human beings is false. It does not follow from the falsehood of the principle that one ought not to steal whisky from alcoholics, that the principle that one ought not to steal is false.

To this an upholder of the scientific conception of morals might reply that I have taken for granted what I am trying to prove. Were I to admit the lawyers' conception of moral rules this difficulty would not arise. But were I to admit the lawyers' conception of moral rules, the lower-order principles would be so careful as to be inane. Once again, no stakes, no winnings.

Supposing it is conceded that in a moral system the *modus tollendo tollens* does not necessarily produce a valid inference. Is anything of the scientific conception of morals worth preserving? In my view, nothing is worth preserving for if a moral system is such that the truth or falsehood of the principles on which one acts are entirely irrelevant to the truth or falsehood of the higher-level principles from which the principles on which one acts are said to be derived, then the higher-level principles can be dismissed as otiose.

SUMMARY : One should reject the scientific conception of morals.

CHAPTER EIGHT

Choice

T HE use of principle is confined to situations in which we have
or may have a choice of what to do. When we are faced with
a situation of choice, we can reach our decision in a number of
distinguishable ways:

(1) We can decide by habit.
We shave when we get up in the morning because it has become
'second nature' to do so. We become 'creatures of habit' when
we refuse to take *any* new decisions and arrange our lives so that
we can always choose to do what we have done before.

(2) We can choose on trust.
When we cannot decide what to do, we may go to someone
else for advice and do what he or she tells us to do. If we cannot
make up our mind which wine to choose at a restaurant, we may
ask the wine waiter for help and choose what he advises. If we
cannot make up our mind whether to go to the university or to a
firm of law crammers before taking our Bar Finals, we may ask
an eminent lawyer for his advice and do what the eminent lawyer
suggests. There is a variety of choosing on trust in which we
delegate the choice: where, e.g., we go to a restaurant and let our
escort take the choices for us and then eat the meal our escort has
chosen.

(3) We can choose 'on balance' of the consequences.
When we go shopping we have choices to make which are
fundamentally of the sort: 'If I spend £x on this article, it will be
mine; but I shall have £x less to spend on other things. Which is
the better?' Insofar as the number of choices an individual makes
can be quantified, we probably make more choices on balance of
the consequences than in any other way.

(4) We can choose arbitrarily.

We can spin a coin to decide, e.g., who shall serve the first game in a tennis match. There is a variety of choosing arbitrarily which is a combination of this and choosing on balance of the consequences which may be called choosing 'on hunch'—when, e.g., we decide to put our money on one particular horse in a race to the exclusion of the others. In such a case we are predicting the consequence that it will win, but on evidence which many would consider to be sketchy.

(5) Situations in which 'circumstances decide' what we shall do. A child born into an English-speaking family 'has no choice' but to speak English; and although we (having had an opportunity of learning to speak another language) may speak of choosing to speak English, or beginning to think in French 'through force of habit'—this is not available to everyone.

All the situations of choice which I have described above are ones in which we are not concerned to improve the way in which we make the choice. We may want to make the correct choice (e.g. in placing bets) but we think we know we cannot improve the *way* in which we make it. In this respect these choices are quite unlike another way in which we may choose, for we may choose *on principle*.

(6) Choosing on principle.

When faced with a choice, we may decide to do one thing rather than another because one *ought* to do so. When we do this we call in aid the school of thought to which we adhere, and lay down guide lines to others.

No difficult choice is ever as simple as those outlined above. If I cannot make up my mind whether to go to Spain or Jugoslavia on my holiday, I have presumably made up my mind not to go where I habitually go. Then I may choose to go to Spain on the advice of my travel agent, or on balance of the consequences because I am afraid of earthquakes in Jugoslavia, or on hunch, or because I have spun a coin to decide, or because I really have no

The Use of Principle

choice, Spain being cheaper and because I have not enough money to go to Jugoslavia, or because my wife wants to go there and I have delegated the choice to her, or on principle that one ought not to support the Fascists in Spain by supplying them with foreign currency. Or there may be any combination of these: I may decide on principle that one ought to delegate the choice of one's holiday to one's wife.

The difference between all the other ways of choosing and the decision made on principle is that there is meant to be a lesson in it *for others*. It is only if I decide not to go to Spain *on principle,* that *you* (if you are in my school of thought) may be affected because you ought not to go to Spain either (or that is my argument). The thing which distinguishes choosing on principle from the others, and makes it important, is that by so choosing we are potentially committing our school of thought as well as ourselves: we are *trying* to make our mark on our population.

SUMMARY: What gives principles their special importance is that a choice made on principle aspires to implicate other people as well as the agent.

Complete Summary

IN classifying human activity, one can distinguish between purposive and aimless behaviour; the distinctive mark of purposive behaviour is that it is directed towards accomplishing tasks, producing results, reaching goals, pursuing ends and achieving ambitions. Speaking is a variety of purposive behaviour. For some people, philosophising is a variety of purposive behaviour directed to the aim of getting clearer on things. To this end, much may depend on how individual words ought to be used.

Purposive behaviour directed towards the same result recurs, both when engaged in by the same person and when engaged in by others. I shall call these recurrences separate performances of the same 'pattern of purposive behaviour'. It is a contingent fact about two performances of the same pattern of purposive behaviour that they can be compared with one another on their success in achieving the result at which the pattern of purposive behaviour is aimed. I shall call a statement of the form set out below a 'confined weak comparison':

COMPARISON (MARK I)

'For agent X, action A is a better way of performing the pattern of purposive behaviour P than action B if he wants to achieve result R in circumstances (1) and (2).'—*Spokesman*.

Statements of this form have the same logic whether they are about earthy or lofty patterns of purposive behaviour.

I will call a weak comparison, in which the agent may be anyone, an 'unconfined weak comparison', to distinguish it from a weak comparison which is peculiar to one particular individual or class of individuals (a 'confined weak comparison'), thus:

COMPARISON (MARK II)

'(For anyone) Action A is a better way of performing the pattern of purposive behaviour P than action B if one wants to achieve result R in circumstances (1) and (2).'—*Spokesman.*

All the more complex verbal constructions used in teaching and learning how to perform patterns of purposive behaviour can be constructed from this one basic posit.

It is false to suggest that it is better not to assign truth-values to value-judgments. Where, in a comparison, the result at which the pattern of purposive behaviour is said to be aimed is too vague to be identifiable, or the alternative actions specified are indistinguishable, then I shall say of such a comparison that it is inane. So comparisons have a three-valued logic. The First Maxim in establishing the truth-value of a comparison is that it it should be assumed to be inane unless it can be established to be true or false.

The Second Maxim is that, when advancing a comparison, one ought to establish its truth-value by showing that the consequences of adopting it would, or would not, conduce to the result at which the particular pattern of purposive behaviour in question is aimed. 'Teleological reasons' (as I shall call these) justify lofty and earthy comparisons alike. The Third Maxim is that when entertaining the idea of using a comparison, one ought to establish its truth or falsehood by taking the word of the experts in the particular pattern of purposive behaviour involved. These are 'received reasons' for thinking a principle to be true or false.

If a spokesman says of an unconfined weak comparison that it is inane, true or false, one ought not to conclude that it is so for everyone in the world. The extent of its universality need only embrace the population likely to be exposed to it. Although the more perplexing philosophical difficulties arise when spokesmen's unconfined weak comparisons conflict with one another, there is virtual unanimity of opinion about unconfined weak comparisons over a wide range of patterns of purposive behaviour.

One may distinguish between Mark II comparisons and more general unconfined weak comparisons (in which few or none of the circumstances are specified). The more general unconfined weak comparisons may be shown thus:

COMPARISON (MARK III)

'Action A is a better way of performing the pattern of purposive behaviour P than action B if one wants to achieve result R.'—*Spokesman.*

A true more specific comparison may not necessarily be validly derivable from the corresponding true more general comparison. A false more specific comparison may not necessarily falsify the corresponding true more general comparison.

One may distinguish between more general forms of unconfined weak comparisons which are 'complete' (as, for instance, the Mark III examples), and those in which the result R is assumed, or taken for granted, or left vague by accident or design. These will be called 'incomplete' and may be shown thus:

COMPARISON (MARK IV)

'Action A is a better way of performing the pattern of purposive behaviour P than action B.'

The truth-value of a comparison may be dependent upon what the result aimed at is; but an incomplete unconfined weak comparison functions perfectly efficiently in our language.

What I shall call a 'strong comparison':

COMPARISON (MARK V)

'Action C is the best way of performing the pattern of purposive behaviour P.'—*Spokesman.*

is incomplete as it stands but can be completed by specifying the result R at which the pattern of purposive behaviour in question is aimed. A Mark V comparison is true if, but only if, action C is better than any other action of which the spokesman is apprised.

In English, that one ought always to perform a pattern of purposive behaviour in the best way, is true by definition. 'Good', 'bad', 'right' and 'wrong' can be defined in terms of 'ought' and 'ought not'.

A spokesman's field of acquaintance is rarely limited to his own experience and insight; he has other people's (notably his parents') knowledge available to him. The urge to reach agreement in one's unconfined comparisons springs from a desire to be able to teach and learn efficiently. This same desire produces a tendency to generalise comparisons which may not be justified. One ought to acknowledge the existence of and the reasons for different schools of thought in performing a pattern of purposive behaviour. Schools of thought spring up to further the efficiency of imparting knowledge from one person to another. 'Principles' ought to be looked upon as unconfined strong comparisons in which the spokesman has been supplanted by the 'school of thought'. Principles are 'complete' when they specify the result at which they are aimed, 'incomplete' when they do not.

Moral principles and others have the same logic. Second-order comparisons—of the form: principle A is more important than principle B—may sometimes be used to resolve conflicts between true principles. A decision as to what (if any) is the master art of all does not solve the question of which are moral principles and which not. When experts conflict in the second-order principles they advocate, one ought not to choose between them on principle.

The distinction between moral principles and others lies in the context in which these respectively occur. One ought to treat a principle as a moral principle in the context where the agent adopts it with no motive. One ought to describe those principles and those principles only which a person usually backs against all comers as his moral principles. They are, by definition, incomplete principles. For anyone, his moral principles are the principles whose truth-value he knows, irrespective of teleological and received reasons. We are frighteningly ignorant of our own motives, and this is why we sometimes mistake for a moral principle (by my definition) something which is really not a moral principle but a means towards an end we had overlooked or deceived ourselves about. Prichard was right in saying that when we act in accordance with a moral principle 'we have no purpose or end'. Man's infinite variety stems from the fact that his moral principles may be unique to himself. All principles can be supported by reasons, but in any school of thought, individuals will adhere to moral principles (or to no moral principles) in a pattern which will approximate closer to a random scatter than to a coherent system.

The prescriptivist account of the language of morals is wrong. One should eschew the lawyers' conception of moral rules. One should reject the scientific conception of morals. What gives principles their special importance is that a choice made on principle aspires to implicate other people as well as the agent.

References

(1) P. B. Medawar. *The Art of the Soluble*. Methuen, London. 1967. p. 133.

(2) Hunter Diack. *Helping at home with reading. Part One—a child learns to speak*. Where? A.C.E. January, 1968.

(3) W. V. Quine. *Word and Object*. Technology Press and Wiley, New York and London. 1960. p. 3.

(4) 'Comparison' is Aaron Sloman's word: How to Derive 'Better' from 'Is'. *American Philosophical Quarterly*. January 1969. p. 43; and 'Ought' and 'Better'. *Mind*. July 1970. p. 385.

(5) W. V. Quine. *Philosophy & Logic*. Prentice-Hall Inc., N.J. 1970.

(6) Gilbert Ryle. *Proceedings of the Aristotelian Society*. Vol. 46. 1946. p. 1.

(7) For 'Description-word' see P. H. Nowell-Smith. *Ethics*. Penguin Books, London. 1954. p. 72.

(8) J. O. Urmson. *The Emotive Theory of Ethics*. Hutchinson, London. 1968. p. 64.

(9) C. D. Broad. *Five Types of Ethical Theory*. Kegan Paul, London. 1930. p. 206.

(10) G. E. Moore. *Principia Ethica*. Cambridge University Press. 1903. para. 91.

(11) Aristotle. *The Nicomachean Ethics*. Translated by J. A. K. Thomson. Penguin Books, Middlesex. 1953. p. 25.

(12) Stuart Hampshire. *Thought and Action*. Chatto and Windus, London. 1959. p. 238.

(13) Aristotle. *Op. cit.* p. 27.

(14) Quoted by L. S. Stebbing. *A Modern Introduction to Logic*. Methuen, London. 4th Edition. 1945. p. 115.

References

(15) William H. Whyte. *The Organisation Man.* Jonathan Cape, London. 1957. p. 382.

(16) H. A. Prichard. *Moral Obligation.* Clarendon Press, Oxford. 1949. pp. 7, 9 and 10.

(17) G. E. Moore. *Op. cit.* p. 188.

(18) Norman Malcolm. *Ludwig Wittgenstein. A Memoir.* Oxford University Press. 1958. p. 39.

(19) Medawar. *Op cit.* p 144.

(20) Urmson. *Op. cit.* p. 69.

(21) R. M. Hare. *The Language of Morals.* Oxford. Clarendon Press. 1952. p. 49.

(22) R. B. Braithwaite. *An Empiricist's View of the Nature of Religious Belief.* Cambridge University Press. 1955.

Index

acquaintance, field of, 56–9, 110
aesthetician's comparison, 20, 49, 53
  principle, 66, 71, 80, 81, 82, 83,
    84, 85, 86
aim, difficulty of definition of, 10–11
aimless behaviour, 9–12, 107
ambitions, achievement requires
    purposive behaviour, 9, 12,
    107
'anyone', 40
apprenticeship, situations of, 57,
    59, 64, 80, 100
arbitrary moral principles, 93–6
Archbishop's comparison, 32
Ardrey, 88
Aristotle, 74, 76, 78
art, master, of all, 75–7, 110
Art Dealer's comparison, 32
Ayer, A. J., 36

'bad', 54–5
Bareau, Paul, 94–5
behaviour, aimless, 9–12, 107
  patterns of purposive, 9–26, 31,
    33–6, 38, 40–1, 43, 47, 52,
    56–8, 60–6, 74–5, 79, 80, 82,
    107–10
  purposive, 9–12, 13, 15, 16, 22,
    74, 107
Braithwaite, R. B., 36, 101, 102
Broad, C. D., 35
Businessman's comparison, 20, 49, 50
  principle, 66, 81, 85–6

choice, 104–6, 111

Christopher Robin's comparison,
  30, 31
Cobbett, William, 63
communication, 14, 40
comparisons, 27–31, 33–8, 39, 44–7,
  50, 52, 61, 67–73, 108–10
  confined weak, 17–24, 26, 107
  incomplete strong, 54, 109
  Mark I, 17–21, 22, 42, 64, 107
  Mark II, 24, 26, 27, 30, 31, 32, 42,
    44, 45, 46, 48, 51, 64, 108–9
  Mark III, 42, 44, 45, 46, 47, 48,
    64, 69, 98, 109
  Mark IV, 47, 48, 49, 50, 51, 54,
    65, 109
  Mark V, 51, 52, 53, 54, 55, 60,
    65, 109
  philosophical, 97
  second order, 72–5, 77,
    110
    strong, 75, 110
  strong, 51–66, 75, 109
  Aesthetician's, 20, 49, 53
  Archbishop's, 32
  Art Dealer's, 32
  Businessman's, 20, 49, 50
  Christopher Robin's, 30, 31
  Dietician's, 18, 42, 48, 50, 52
  Englishman abroad's, 23
  Etymologist's, 18, 24, 34, 42,
    48, 52
  Law Tutor's, 19, 34, 44, 45, 48,
    50, 53, 60
  Logical Positivist's, 19, 21, 27,
    28, 36, 49, 53, 56, 60
  Loyalist's, 30
  Mechanic's, 19, 21, 43, 48, 53, 60
  Musicologist's, 20, 21, 49, 53,

comparisons cont.
  Nanny's, 18, 24, 34, 41, 42, 48,
    52, 60, 72
  Prince of Wales's, 23
  Probation Officer's, 19, 49, 71
  Rosicrucians, 31
  Traditionalist's, 30
  true, 61, 108
  truth-value of, 27–40, 44, 50, 61,
    109
  unconfined, 61–2, 64
    strong, 53, 66, 110
    weak, 22–50, 107–9
  weak, 15–27, 39, 107
    complete unconfined, 47–50,
      109
    general unconfined, 41–6, 109
    incomplete unconfined, 47–50,
      109
    specific unconfined, 41–6, 109
complete principles, 66, 110
complete summary, 107–11
complete unconfined weak comparisons, 47–50, 109
conception, lawyer's of moral rules,
    100, 111
  scientific of morals, 101–3, 111
conduct, often purposeless, 11
  when purposive or pointless, 11
confined weak comparisons, 17–24,
    26, 107
conflicts between experts, 78–9,
    108
  true principles, 74–5, 110
'consensus', 61
consequences, 34–5

decision to 'back' a principle, 85–7,
    110
description-words, 27
Diack, Hunter, 13
Dietician's comparison, 18, 42, 48,
    50, 52
  principle, 65, 68
drive for truth and generality, 60–2

ends, their pursuit requires purposive behaviour, 9, 12, 107
Englishman abroad's comparison, 23
ethics, prescriptive theory of, 97–9,
    111
etymologist's comparison, 18, 24,
    34, 42, 48, 52
  principle, 65
experts, conflicts between, 78–9, 108

field of acquaintance, 56–9, 110
first maxim, 33, 68, 108
Freud, S., 88

general unconfined weak comparisons, 41–6, 109
generality and truth, 60–2
goals, to reach requires purposive
  behaviour, 9, 12, 107
'good', 54, 55
Goodman, 36

Hallidie Smith, Canon H. H. M., 95
Hampshire, Stuart, 75
Hare, R. M, 8, 36, 99, 100
Hunter Diack, 13

ignorance of our motives, 87–9, 110
importance of motive, 80–4
'inane', 31, 33, 108
inanity, 29–33
'inanity', two sorts of, 29–33
incomplete principles, 66, 87, 110
incomplete strong comparisons, 54,
    109
incomplete unconfined weak comparisons, 47–50, 109
inference, 21, 28
inference, principles of, 21, 45, 46

'knowledge', 25

Index

language of morals, prescriptivist
account of, 99, 111
Law Tutor's comparison, 19, 34,
44, 45, 48, 50, 53, 60
principle, 65, 69
Lawyer's conception of moral
rules, 100, 111
learning, looking involves, 13
to see, 12-13
Leavis, Mr. & Mrs., 60
Lincoln, Abraham, 68
logic, 21, 22, 33, 110
Logical Positivist's comparison, 19,
21, 27, 28, 36, 49, 53, 56, 60
principle, 65
looking, talking and philosophising,
12-15
Loyalist's comparison, 30

Malcolm, N., 36, 96
Mark I comparisons, 17-21, 22, 42,
64, 107,
Mark II comparisons, 24, 26, 27, 30,
31, 32, 42, 44, 45, 46, 48, 51,
64, 108-9
Mark III comparisons, 42, 44, 45,
46, 47, 48, 64, 69, 98, 109
Mark IV comparisons, 47, 48, 49,
50, 51, 54, 65, 109
Mark V comparisons, 51, 52, 53, 54,
55, 60, 65, 109
Master art of all, 75-7, 110
Maxim, First, 33, 68, 108
Second, 34, 35, 68, 108
Third, 36, 37, 38, 68, 108
Maxims, 39, 108
Mechanic's comparison, 19, 21, 43,
48, 53, 60
principle, 65 74
Medawar, P. B., 13, 97
Mitford, Nancy, 58
modus ponendo ponens, 44, 45
modus tollendo tollens, 45, 101, 102,
103
Moore, G. E., 52, 78, 90

'moral', 75
moral philosophy, 26, 89-92
principle, 7, 67-72, 75, 110-11
principles, 7, 47, 75, 77, 80-96,
110-11
principles, arbitrary, 93-6
rules, lawyer's conception of,
100-1
morals, language of, 99, 111
scientific conception of, 101-3,
111
motive, implies purposive
behaviour, 10
motives, ignorance of our, 87-9,
110
importance of, 80-4
Musicologist's comparison, 20, 21,
49, 53
principle, 66, 69-70, 71

Nanny's comparison, 18, 24, 34, 41,
42, 48, 52, 60, 72
principle, 65
no-falsehoods principle, 81-4

Orwell, George, 72-3, 78
'ought', 54, 55

patterns of purposive behaviour,
9-26, 31, 33-6, 38, 40-1, 43,
47, 52, 56-8, 60-6, 74-5, 79,
80, 82, 107-110,
performance, 17, 21, 22, 107
philosophical comparisons, 97
philosophising, looking and talking,
12-15
philosophy, 14, 15
moral, 26, 89-92
Popper, 36
'population', 40, 62
posit, definition, 7
pragmatists, 35
prairie oyster, recipe, 18

preface, 7–8
prescriptive theory of ethics, 97–9,
    111
Pritchard, H. A., 89–90, 93
Prince of Wales's comparison, 23
principle, moral, 7, 67–72, 75,
    110–11
    Aesthetician's, 66, 71, 80, 81,
        82, 83, 84, 85, 86
    Businessman's, 66, 81, 85–6
    decision to 'back', 85–7, 110
    Dieticians, 65, 68
    Etymologist's, 65
    Law Tutor's, 65, 69
    Logical Positivist's, 65
    Mechanic's, 65, 74
    Musicologist's, 66, 69–70, 71
    Nanny's, 65
    no-falsehood, 81–2, 83, 84
    of inference, 21, 45, 46
    Probation Officer's, 65
    use of, 104–6
principles, 61, 64–79, 110
    complete, 66, 110
    incomplete, 66, 87, 110
    moral, 7, 47, 75, 77, 80–96,
        110–11
    arbitrary, 93–6
    of inference, 69–72
    Principle 1, 69–70
    Principle 2, 69–70
    Principle 3, 71
    Principle 4, 71
    Principle 5, 71
    second order, 78–9, 110
    true, conflicts between, 74–5
Probation Officer's comparison, 19,
    49, 71
principle, 65
purpose, difficulty of definition, 10
purposive behaviour, 9–12, 13, 15,
    16, 22, 74, 107
    patterns of, 9–26, 31, 33–6, 38,
        40–1, 43, 47, 52, 56–8,
        60–6, 74–5, 79, 80, 82,
        107–110

Quine, W. V., 7, 14, 25, 36, 51

reasons, teleological, 33–5, 108
    received, 35–8
received reasons, 35–8
results, to produce requires purpos-
    ive behaviour, 9, 12, 16, 107
'right', 54, 55
rival theories, 97–103
Rosicrucian's comparison, 31
Russell, Bertrand, 58
Ryle, Gilbert, 25, 36

schools of thought, 62–4, 110
scientific conception of morals,
    101–3, 111
second maxim, 34, 35, 68, 108
second order comparisons, 72–5,
    77, 110
    principles, 78–9, 110
    strong, 75, 110
Shakespeare, William, 73, 78
Shawe-Taylor, Desmond, 58, 99
sight, learning how to use, 12
situations of apprenticeship, 57,
    59, 64, 80, 100
Sloman, Aaron, 47
speaking, a variety of purposive
    behaviour, 15, 107
specific unconfined weak compari-
    sons, 41–6, 109
speech, 14
standards, 34
Stevenson, C. L., 8
Strawson, 36
strong comparisons, 51–66, 75, 109
    incomplete, 54, 109
    second order, 75, 110
    unconfined, 53, 66, 110
strong second order comparisons,
    75, 110
summary, complete, 107–11

talking, looking and philosophising,
    12–15

Index

teleological reasons, 33–5, 108
theories, rival, 97–103
theory, prescriptive of ethics, 97–9, 111
third maxim, 36, 37, 38, 68, 108
Thomas, Harford, 72
thought, schools of, 62–4, 110
Toulmin, S. E., 8
tradition, 63
traditionalist's comparison, 30
true comparisons, 61, 108
  principles, conflicts between, 74–5
truth and generality, 60–2
truth-value of comparisons, 27–40, 44, 50, 61, 109

unconfined comparisons, 61–2, 64
unconfined strong comparisons, 53, 66, 110
  weak comparisons, 22–50, 107–9
    complete, 47, 109
    general, 41–6, 109
    incomplete, 47–50, 109
    specific, 41–6, 109
universality, 39, 50

Urmson, J. O., 34, 98
use of principle, 104–6
utilitarians, 35

value-judgement, 27, 28, 108

weak comparisons, 15–27, 39, 107
  complete unconfined, 47, 109
  confined, 17–24, 26, 107
  general unconfined, 41–6, 109
  incomplete, unconfined, 47–50, 109
  unconfined, 22–50, 107–9
    specific, 41–6, 109
Whitehead, 88
Whyte, W. H., 88
Wisdom, John, 36, 97
Wittgenstein, L., 96
words, use of, 14, 15
'wrong', 54, 55

Young, J. Z., 13